21 BLACK FUTURES
THE ANTHOLOGY

OBSIDIAN THEATRE COMPANY

PLAYWRIGHTS CANADA PRESS
TORONTO

First edition: October 2023
Printed and bound in Canada by Imprimerie Gauvin, Gatineau

Jacket art and design by Yung Yemi

Playwrights Canada Press
202-269 Richmond St. w., Toronto, ON M5V 1X1
416.703.0013 | info@playwrightscanada.com | www.playwrightscanada.com

LIBRARY AND ARCHIVES CANADA CATALOGUING IN PUBLICATION
Title: 21 black futures : the anthology / Obsidian Theatre Company.
Other titles: Twenty-one black futures
Names: Obsidian Theatre Company.
Description: Plays.
Identifiers: Canadiana (print) 20230454526 | Canadiana (ebook) 2023045464X
| ISBN 9780369104557 (softcover) | ISBN 9780369104571 (EPUB) | ISBN 9780369104564 (PDF)
Subjects: LCSH: Canadian drama—Black authors. | LCSH: Canadian drama—21st century.
| CSH: Canadian drama (English)—Black Canadian authors.
| CSH: Canadian drama (English)—21st century.
Classification: LCC PS8307 .A121 2023 | DDC C812/.6080896071—dc23

Playwrights Canada Press operates on land which is the current and ancestral home of the Anishinaabe Nations (Ojibwe / Chippewa, Odawa, Potawatomi, Algonquin, Saulteaux, Nipissing, and Mississauga), the Wendat, and the members of the Haudenosaunee Confederacy (Mohawk, Oneida, Onondaga, Cayuga, Seneca, and Tuscarora), as well as Metis and Inuit peoples. It always was and always will be Indigenous land.

We acknowledge the financial support of the Canada Council for the Arts, the Ontario Arts Council (OAC), Ontario Creates, the Government of Ontario, and the Government of Canada for our publishing activities.

Canada Council for the Arts | Conseil des arts du Canada
ONTARIO ARTS COUNCIL
CONSEIL DES ARTS DE L'ONTARIO
an Ontario government agency
un organisme du gouvernement de l'Ontario
ONTARIO CREATES | ONTARIO CRÉATIF
Canada
Ontario

To our future storytellers.

CONTENTS

CONTENTS

A RADICAL OFFERING IN UNPRECEDENTED TIMES: THE STORY OF *21 BLACK FUTURES*

It was July 2020 when I began my journey as the new artistic director of Obsidian Theatre, a twenty-year-old company with a strong legacy of centring and championing Black stories and Black artists. We were in the midst of a pandemic and a renewed global attention to anti-Black racism. Theatres across the country were shut down, and the future of live performance was uncertain.

To say it was quite a time to begin my journey as an artistic director is an understatement.

All the programming my predecessor Philip Akin had planned for his final season was cancelled or postponed. I was in the position of not only learning a new job, but also developing material for the 2020–2021 season. I had the choice to either wait until the pandemic subsided, or adapt and create new programming that would reflect our times in both form and content.

Prior to beginning my role at Obsidian, I was a busy freelance theatre director and independent producer who had also seen all of my upcoming gigs disappear due to COVID-19. With no end to the pandemic in sight, I went further into self-isolation, mourning privately the continuous murder of Black people at the hands of police. With no access to the theatre and no access to community, I was hurting and in need of connection.

I wondered how other Black artists across the country were doing. Especially when, around the world, the gaze of institutions, individuals, and even politicians had turned sharply toward us. How could I respond and support Black artists from an institutional capacity? I thought about all the veteran artists who had been part of building Obsidian's legacy and the aspiring theatre-makers, in various parts of the country, who had maybe never even heard of Obsidian. Was there a way we could come together in this moment and create something communal and unapologetically Black; something with the Black gaze at its centre? A radical offering in unprecedented times.

I was interested in new stories about imagined Black futures to counter the messaging that was suddenly everywhere about us, but not from us. I was interested in new words, in new language, in what Black writers and thinkers across the country had to say about our future.

In conversation with the team at Obsidian, we decided to engage twenty-one writers from different generations and with different levels of experience—writers who reflected the rich diversity of Blackness in Canada. Twenty-one to celebrate Obsidian's twenty-first anniversary in 2021. Each writer was tasked with writing a ten-minute monodrama—a one-person play—in response to the question: What is the future of Blackness? We further engaged twenty-one Black directors and twenty-one Black actors to bring these stories to life as short theatrical films. Our goal was to give as many opportunities to as many diverse Black artists as possible and to bring new voices together from both film and theatre. It was a grand experiment to create as rich a tapestry as we could for the imagining of Black futures.

The experiment finally came to life. The journey to get there—to create and present work of that scale in the middle of a pandemic—was certainly not easy. We learned a ton, adapted daily to producing a new form of storytelling that was a hybrid of theatre and film, and met and connected with so many incredible Black artists in a way that had never happened before at Obsidian. We are proud of and grateful to the sixty-three Black artists and creative and production teams who worked tirelessly for months to make this project happen. We celebrate their incredible talent.

All of us at Obsidian are truly grateful for the partnership with the CBC, which gave us a national platform to present this work. A special thanks to our supervising producer, Lucius Dechausay, who was an incredible collaborator, helping us shape the filming of this project with so much rigour and care. Huge thanks to our venue production partner, TO Live, for giving us a space to film the project, and to all our donors and community supporters who have helped us make this project possible.

Thank you to the team at Obsidian, who were a rock during this process. To my predecessors Philip Akin and Alison Sealy-Smith, thank you for the strong foundation you left at Obsidian, which we are now building upon.

Looking back at the creation of these pieces three years later, I am amazed by how timeless they feel. In many ways the idea of imagining and reimagining the future is part of our creative lineage as Black storytellers. We are constantly trying to marry the past, present, and future through movements such as Afro-futurism and Afro-surrealism in an attempt to fight against systemic oppression and erasure. My hope is that this anthology will inspire future generations of storytellers all across Canada and beyond to continue this creative lineage and to never settle for dominant narratives.

What is the future of Blackness? Read the anthology now for twenty-one versions of it.

Mumbi Tindyebwa Otu
Artistic Director, Obsidian Theatre Company

SEASON 1

Season 1 of *21 Black Futures* was produced by Obsidian Theatre Company and CBC Arts, and was first aired on CBC Gem on February 12, 2021.

The Death News by Amanda Parris

The Sender by Cheryl Foggo

Jah in the Ever-Expanding Song by Kaie Kellough

Beyere by Shauntay Grant

Madness With Rocks by Peace Akintade-Oluwagbeye

Witness Shift by Donna-Michelle St. Bernard

Sensitivity by Lawrence Hill

THE DEATH NEWS

AMANDA PARRIS

Performer: Lovell Adams-Gray
Director: Charles Officer

This play is dedicated to my son Malcolm, who was huddled safe in my belly while I wrote these words.

ACKNOWLEDGEMENTS

Thank you to Kevin for taking such good care of me always, but particularly in 2020 as I carried our child in the midst of a pandemic and a cultural reckoning and wrote these words. Thank you to my mum for always believing in and encouraging my writing. Thank you to Mumbi Tindyebwa Otu for inviting me on this journey. Thank you to Myekah for your patience and insightful questions that helped unravel the characters and the story. Thank you to Charles, Lovell, and the entire *21 Black Futures* production crew for bringing life to these words.

ABOUT THE PLAYWRIGHT

Amanda Parris is a writer, TV host, and producer. Amanda is the creator and showrunner of the comedy series *Revenge of the Black Best Friend*. It won the 2023 Canadian Screen Award for Best Web Program and was an official selection at the 2022 CANNESERIES Festival. Her play *Other Side of the Game* was awarded the 2019 Governor General's Literary Award for Drama, and her short play *The Death News* won the 2022 Canadian Screen Award for Best Writing. Last year, Amanda received the inaugural Changemaker Award from the Canadian Screen Awards and earlier this year she was awarded the ACTRA Sandi Ross Award for her efforts to call out systemic racism in the Canadian media community.

ARTIST NOTE

The Death News invites Black people to record their obituaries using their own authentic voices and words to illustrate their lives. On first read, this revolutionary and absurd concept, written by Amanda Parris, moved me to my core and as a Black man.

The power of the piece is the call to action: for us Black people to claim our existence, claim our narrative.

In the play, the struggle for Dante lies in answering the question: What do you want people to remember about you? His journey leads to understanding what matters to him the most.

True say, the brutal evidence of racial injustice we witnessed as a Black community in 2020 was unforgettable. I can't say there is anything more essential to examine for us. Tomorrow is not promised.

—Charles Officer, Director

CHARACTERS

Kiena Kifo
Dante Cooper

Interior. The Death News *set—day.*

Open on KIENA *Kifo, a forty-seven-year-old broadcast journalist and the host, creator, and executive producer of* The Death News. *She is seated at her desk on set. She looks straight into the camera and addresses her audience.*

KIENA: In this world, at this time, premature Black death is an inevitability. Will you idly sit and wait for it to come? Or will you define the story that is told about the time that you were here? Welcome to *The Death News.*

KIENA *transitions into* DANTE *Cooper, a thirty-one-year-old manager at a telemarketing company and former rapper, producer, and clothing line entrepreneur from the west end of Toronto.*

Interior. Bedroom—night.

DANTE *is in his bedroom, staring at his reflection in the mirror but not really seeing himself. Lost in thought, he suddenly blinks and comes back to the present moment.*

DANTE: This is stupid. I look stupid. What does one wear to deliver their final words to the world? I guess pre-recording my obituary would fall under the category of special occasion but . . . am I supposed to wear a tux or . . . do I just dress like me? Fuck, Dante, you're moving like a gyal. Just make a decision and go fam.

Kisses his teeth.

I don't even know why I'm doing this. I mean, I know why, but . . . maybe I should reschedule. Yeah. I'm just not feeling this. I don't think today is the right day . . .

KIENA: *(voice-over)* I've been asked a lot about my passion for these pre-recorded obituaries.

DANTE: All right, all right. I got this. Okay. How about this tie?

Pause.

Nina always liked this tie . . .

Nah. This ain't it.

He takes off the tie aggressively.

I don't know what to wear. I don't even know what to say. I have the power to tell my own story but . . . which story do I tell? It's not like life is a timeline—beginning, middle, and end. There's different versions, different points of view. Even in my own mind.

DANTE transitions into KIENA.

Interior. The Death News *set—day.*

KIENA: I'll tell you why I keep allocating so much time to what "critics" call this morbid element. For generations Black people in this country—and beyond—have entrusted their narratives to a media industry that has failed them. THEY told only one version of us. THEY summarized our lives into clickbait headlines. THEY simplified our stories into one-note stereotypes. But that was then. Today, because of *The Death News*, THEY no longer have the power.

KIENA transitions into DANTE.

Interior. Bedroom—night. DANTE is still trying on clothes.

DANTE: But . . . what if I am a stereotype? Is it like . . . irresponsible to tell my story then? Do I leave out my single mum and my high-rise building? My low-income neighbourhood and how I got caught up in the game as a yute? Fuck that. That's me.

It's not all of me but it's part of my truth . . . I dunno, man.

KIENA: *(voice-over)* Here on *The Death News*, we invite Black people to record their own obituaries using their own authentic voices, choosing their own words to construct the final picture of their lives.

DANTE: And what the fuck is an authentic voice? Should I bring my *(clears throat, straightens back)* professional work voice or my *(slouches, starts to sway)* how I spit on the block voice? Which version makes the cut? One that'll make my mum proud or the one that the man 'dem will know and recognize?

He looks back in the mirror.

This is a definite no.

KIENA: *(voice-over)* Premature Black death is an unswaying truth that prevails year after year. Now that you know that truth, what are you going to do with it? Will you sit idly and wait for it to come? Or will you grab the reins and define the story that is told about the time that you were here?

DANTE: She says it like it's so simple. Like what am I gonna talk about? The fact that I love to make the homies laugh? True say I do take that shit serious. And when I say laugh, I mean like really laugh. You know to the point where their eyes get real small and they're struggling to breathe? But like in the good way, not in the racist cop on your neck kinda way? I'm not saying I'm a comedian or nothing. I just . . . I dunno. I love to see the homies laugh. But that ain't somethin' to say in an obit.

I need something inspiring. Like a phrase people will want to quote on the gram. It looked so easy when I saw Nina do it.

She made everything look easy. Even when she was struggling. She never let it show. And everything she did seemed perfect. Well except singing. Bruh, that female couldn't hold a note. But everything else was perfect. Even the way she folded clothes was like performance art. Her lines were immaculate. She'd get downright boasty when she would do that final smoothing out. It was mad cute. Nina would know what I should say. These shoes could work.

KIENA: *(voice-over)* The question to ask yourself when constructing your pre-taped obituary: "What do you want people to remember about you?"

DANTE: See now that's one of them questions that seem easy but are hard as fuck 'cause like it depends on the situation. If I knew how I . . . you know like the circumstances . . . of how I'm gonna go? It might be easier. I dunno. Man, this shit is exhausting. Constantly having to consider everything from every angle. I'm tired. Like bone-deep tired of it. The shit I deal with every day, the shit we, Black people deal with every day like racism, classism, microaggressions, police aggressions, the education system, the healthcare system, just everything with this whole Babylon shit-stem. It has an impact on the cellular level you know? I might have lived thirty-one years on this planet but biologically? In my bones? My cells are moving like I'm already sixty-three. It's some crazy shit.

DANTE transitions into KIENA.

Interior. The Death News *set—day.*

KIENA: On tonight's episode of *The Death News*, we highlight the story of Nina Winsome. In her words she was—a publicist, a Leo, and an event planner who loved a well-made martini and watching ridiculous amounts of HGTV. Nina passed away last week after collapsing at work. She leaves behind her mother Naomi, her father Nigel, her sister Nadine, and her pet cat Artemis.

KIENA transitions into DANTE.

Interior. Bedroom—night.

DANTE continues trying on clothes.

KIENA: *(voice-over)* As a subscriber to our Premium Package, Nina pre-scheduled her final pinned tweet. It premieres right now on the platform. Nina's final tweet reads: "Cry for me but don't let them lie about me. They worked me to death. But I was never made to be their mule. My spirit deserves to be free. And now it is."

DANTE: Nina knew her life meant something. And that's why she did the obit. Why the hell did we end again? I can't even remember. I do remember what we had. That peaceful love. That grounded love. Still can't believe I lived that shit. But then of course I had to go and fuck it up. It's just this, this voice began whispering to me, "Hey fam, you see this thing right here . . . this thing can't last. It never lasts for mans like you. And you ain't no exception to the rule."

So, I had to end it. Before it ended me. Before it took down all my defenses.

Left me out in the world vulnerable in a way no Black man ain't got no right to be. Yeah. It had to end. And now she's gone.

KIENA: *(voice-over)* Later in the show we'll be airing our Black-only grieving special—so, Black viewers, have your passcode ready. But first, here is another pre-taped obituary. This time from Dante Cooper.

Interior. The Death News *set—night.*

DANTE: If you're watching this, it means I took my last breath recently. I had a feeling it was gonna happen soon. Not for any particular reason. Just . . . a feeling. But anyway. I don't want my final message to the world to focus on death. I want it to be about life. At the end of the day, I ain't under no illusions. I know that I'm not—or I guess I wasn't—extraordinary. I don't have any amazing talents. I never won no big awards. Didn't travel to no crazy places or create no memorable art. I had my little dreams. But there is something I did do that I want remembered. I loved hard. Like with my whole heart. And I was loved back. By my mum dukes, by the man 'dem who would ride with me to the end . . . and by Nina. Nina Winsome, whose love I may not have deserved but who made me a better person. I loved hard. And that's important because I want it known and on record that I didn't go through this life numb. They may have thrown all the craziest obstacles my way but despite it all, I still felt the deepest shit you can feel. And even if that was the only thing I'd done with my life, isn't that worth grieving? I guess I'm just hoping that my existence won't be dismissed. But yeah. That's it. That's all I wanted to say. Thanks for listening. Have fun breathing.

KIENA: *(voice-over)* That was Dante Cooper, who passed away on Friday at the age of thirty-one. Just a quick reminder that for a limited time only, *The Death News* is offering a 20% off discount for post-mortem wedding ceremonies. Visit our website for more info. And remember, THEY may shape the circumstances of our lives, but THEY can no longer determine the stories that define our lives. Our pain is no longer available for their consumption.

End.

THE SENDER

CHERYL FOGGO

Performer: Amanda Cordner
Director: Leah-Simone Bowen

This is for us.

ACKNOWLEDGEMENTS

I would like to thank Leah Simone-Bowen for her intelligent direction, and Amanda Cordner for her brilliant performance as Cil in the original production of this play.

I would also like to acknowledge Mumbi Tindyebwa Otu and the entire team at Obsidian Theatre Company for creating the unprecedented project that is *21 Black Futures.*

PLAYWRIGHT'S NOTE

In my vision of the future where *The Sender* is set, a global project to eliminate racism and its associated effects has resulted in a world that is peaceful, logical, and sustainable.

ABOUT THE PLAYWRIGHT

Cheryl Foggo is a multiple-award-winning playwright, author, and filmmaker, whose work over the last thirty years has focused on the lives of western Canadians of African descent. Recent works include the NFB feature documentary *John Ware Reclaimed*, as well as the thirtieth anniversary edition of her book *Pourin' Down Rain: A Black Woman Claims Her Place in the Canadian West*. Her plays *Heaven* and *John Ware Reimagined* have received multiple productions in recent years, including at the Citadel in Edmonton, Lunchbox Theatre in Calgary, at the Blyth Theatre Festival, and in Ottawa at the National Arts Centre. Cheryl was the recipient of the Lieutenant Governor of Alberta Distinguished Artist Award; the Doug and Lois Mitchell Outstanding Calgary Artist Award; and the Arts, Media and Entertainment Award from the Calgary Black Chambers, all in 2021. In 2022 she was inducted into the Alberta Order of Excellence.

ARTIST NOTE

2020 marked the thirtieth anniversary of Cheryl Foggo's groundbreaking book *Pourin' Down Rain: A Black Woman Claims Her Place in the Canadian West*. In it, she recounts her life growing up as a Black girl in Calgary with her family, documenting the long legacy that Black people imprinted on the province of Alberta. She wrote the book with the understanding that the Black experience in Alberta had for years been obfuscated by the dominant settler narrative—stories that erased Indigenous nations, Black people, and other people of colour in favour of tales of "open land."

When her book was released in 1990, I was a young Black girl growing up with my family in Edmonton. I had no inkling that a rich history of Black Albertans even existed. I made the false assumption that Black people had arrived around the '50s or '60s because I had never been taught otherwise and could not fathom there were women like Cheryl, whose family had been in Alberta for generations. Because of writers like her, I grew to learn I was not an anomaly, but part of a larger fellowship of Black people in the Prairies, with a rich tapestry of stories and traditions of their own that dated back to the early 1900s.

When Obsidian asked me to be a part of this project and told me it would be Cheryl Foggo's piece I would be directing, it reminded me of a saying: "If one does not see themselves in history, they cannot envision themselves in the future." And so, what a gift it has been to direct a piece about a Black future by the woman who gave me mine.

—Leah-Simone Bowen, Director

CHARACTER

Lucille "Cil" Brown: a Black woman

SETTING

An office space in the future

Interior office space. Day.

CIL is seated at her monitor. There is a large, raised red button at her desk, clearly visible.

She stretches, the end of a long work day. A pleasant tone sounds, indicating her System has logged in.

She touches a device in her ear.

CIL: Hey, System.

Yep, pretty straightforward. The couple that ran the Rights for Whites website tried to smuggle a bunch of music.

Ya, no doubt.

Other than that, smooth as glass. Oh, except I had one weird glitch a couple hours ago.

Like a power surge or something. Maybe ask maintenance to schedule a scan of my LX tonight.

So just one more for today, right?

Do I have his data?

A sound indicates a file's been uploaded to her monitor. She gives it a quick scan.

Got it. He's Implicit Consent with a Code 3 Complaint.

Go ahead and upsync us. Talk to you later.

A sound indicates System's departure.

Good afternoon, twenty-six-year-old Terrance Knight.

This is Transport Room 5.

Mr. Knight, I understand you have lodged a complaint relating to the diagnosis of cataracts in your left eye prior to signing the terms that will enable your transfer to White Supremacist Island.

The Board of Compassionate Exemptions and Extensions has reviewed and denied your complaint.

No.

That has nothing to do with me. Completely different department.

Now I can assure you, cataract surgery is available on White Supremacist Island.

True, the procedure that utilizes the Laserphaco Probe will not be avail . . .

Not negotiable.

If you would . . .

It's . . .

She lifts a hand and raises her voice.

Mr. Knight!

I am authorized to offer advice at my discretion, therefore I will take a moment to point out that your attempt to shout over my communication is a symptom of your chronic interrupting and multi-splaining. This behaviour is even unpopular on White Supremacist Island and there are a lot of quick-tempered people over there. Consider yourself warned.

The Laserphaco Probe is subject to Statute 43.

Residents of White Supremacist Island forfeit all inventions, improvements, and popular entertainments that can be directly linked to Indigenous, Black, or Persons of Colour. The Laserphaco Probe is a patented invention by Patricia Bath, a Black woman.

You'll get the other cataract surgery once you get over there and it'll probably be fine. *Plus,* look at everything else you're getting! No, I know you haven't signed yet, but just hypothetically.

The luxury high-rise includes a built-in gaming wall, ion-factor surround sound, and a dishwasher. Since you're not a voluntary you can't have the three-bedroom, but I'll get you two plus den with a bath-and-a-half. There's an infinity pool and virtual forest sauna on the twenty-second floor.

Well sure, there's always fine print.

The elevators are not equipped with the automatic closing doors that include the flexible belt improvement patented by Alexander Miles, a Black man. This does mean there is increased risk of falling down the elevator shaft, so getting up to the pool is . . . Well, the staircases are safe!

The island has a temperate climate. There are jobs. The beaches are . . .

> *Her station glitches. The lights dim briefly. We hear a powerful rush of water, a whooshing sound. When the lights come back up, a few console lights are flashing.*

(to herself) What's happening?

Mr. Knight! Are you still there?

> CIL *presses her ear device, attempting to summon System 11-14.*

System! System 11-14!

What's going on?

> *She's on her feet now. She repeatedly taps the device in her ear.*

System 11-14 this is Cil.

This is Cil in Sending Room 5. Are you there? I'm having an issue!

She presses the ear device again.

(confused) Who is this?

A long beat as she squints at her monitor and strains to hear.

Who?

Brittany who? Bree?

Bree Corbett!?

CIL drops into her chair, leans forward to get a better look. She taps her ear device again.

System 11-14, I've been hacked! Subject Terrance Knight's briefing was aborted before he could sign and he's been transported. I'm requesting a retrieval for signature.

Bree, shut up! I'm trying to get my . . .

She's still trying to get her System back.

What?

You got his signature? How? What are you . . . ?

I can hardly hear you. My CPU is really unstable. Just a sec.

Okay that's better. Why do you have my transfer's signature and why are you here?! How did you . . .

Terrance Knight is Terry Thane?

Oh my God. Don't tell me you're still seeing Terry Thane.

How did you get him past my System? I'm not supposed to process files of people I know. A name change shouldn't have fooled it.

Wow. You're still as brilliant as ever I see. Stupidest smart person I've ever known.

I didn't recognize him at all. He looks terrible. Okay, give me the signature. Put it up on the Driver Glide and I can scan it to the . . .

She glances at her timer.

But I don't have time! My shift ends in fifteen minutes and if I don't have it in by end of day it doesn't count! Which you well know from when you worked in Tech and Design!

You'll get me two signatures in exchange for a favour? Who's the other signature? Terry was my last file of the day.

What? Why? I thought you still had six months to go in rehab.

She brings up Bree's file.

I've got your file up here and . . . dang. Terrible.

Out of the ten precepts of Racism Elimination 101 your scores are dismal on three of them.

Precept 2—Defending the words or actions of racists by saying "I'm sure they didn't mean it that way."

5—Telling a racialized friend about a racist thing someone said behind their back but refusing to name the perp.

7—Expecting your racialized friends to tolerate your racist partner.

Oof, obviously still doing that.

Okay, this is bad but you've got six months to pull up your scores. Do you really want to spend the rest of your life on White Supremacist Island with him?

All right. Well, that's your choice. You know transfer is binding, right?

You can never come back.

What are the perks you're looking for? No promises, but if I can get them for you I will.

You're 100% on this? You know that the end of sustainable life over there is outside our jurisdiction?

I don't know, I'm just. I guess I hoped for better, from you and for you.

Bree. Girl.

Remember when Terry was working at Lineco? And Asif got the promotion Terry thought he should have had? Remember how angry he was when he came over to your place? Ya, we were in the middle of a Janelle Monáe dance party.

Anyway, Terry was looking for affirmation and you told him Asif seemed pretty brilliant?

Ya. He punched a hole in the wall. Does he still pull shit like that?

I know it's none of my business.

I'm only saying that just because he's not going to have Brown folks to blame for all his problems over there doesn't mean he's going to stop punching holes in walls.

Shrugs in surrender, looks at her timer.

Okay, we don't have much time, what do you want?

She types out Bree's list.

Uh-huh. Right. What colour?

For how long? Okay, it's yours.

That'll be tough, those options are usually reserved for voluntaries. Although, I guess you're technically a voluntary, even though you hacked my station. Fine, I think I can get that.

What else?

Nope, that I cannot do. Cool Sports Network is not possible.

Because it includes Basketball, Football, Soccer, Track and Field, and all the other sports that are dependent on majority labour of Black or Brown people. Statute 6, you've read the agreement. I can give you Relaxation Romps Network. It's got a bunch of stuff—curling, lawn bowling, darts, poker, it's still got the NHL, for now. That's the best I can do.

Is that everything?

She taps some buttons on her screen, we hear a send sound.

Done.

All right, load those signatures.

We hear a sound and two pages drop into CIL's hands. She reads them.

She looks at Bree.

Very funny, Bree. Signed "What's her name" and "Who's-it."

All right. One down, one to go.

Brace yourself. It doesn't hurt but it's cold and wet.

Just what I said. One down—Terry Thane, also known as Terrance Knight. One to go—Brittany Corbett, also known as my former friend.

I don't need your signature, you gave verbal consent. Verbal and Implicit are now valid. I mean we always want signatures where possible, but it's not a requirement anymore. Think of signatures like trophies.

No, he really is gone, Bree. Permanently.

Dead serious. You're actually the one that hit send when you hacked in, which is unfortunate because I find it deeply satisfying to punt the Terries.

Stop it. Oh for . . . there's a box of tissues behind you.

I wouldn't even if I could.

Well look at it from my perspective.

A pleasant tone indicates CIL's System has checked in.

Hey, System 11-14. No, I'm okay. Thanks for asking. It's fine, don't worry. See you tomorrow.

System tones out. Without skipping a beat, CIL carries on with what she was saying to Bree.

No it wasn't. I was genuinely hoping you would choose to go back to rehab. I wanted you to save yourself.

Anyway.

She stands.

I am going to honour all the things you asked for. And I've added a couple more perks. The tire voucher on Terry's truck is upgraded to the really fat ones, and I'll give you some vintage New England Patriots merch from back in the day. Old time's sake.

She pushes the red send button.

We hear a mighty rush of water and a whooshing sound.

Bye, Bree.

End.

JAH IN THE EVER-EXPANDING SONG

KAIE KELLOUGH

Performer: Ravyn Wngz
Director: d'bi.young anitafrika

PLAYWRIGHT'S NOTE

This work was inspired by the song "Every Dub Shall Scrub," by Scientist. That song was originally supposed to play at the beginning to set the mood for the work, but since there may be copyright complications, I would urge anyone reading this to listen to the song, to live with the song for some time. "Every Dub Shall Scrub" provides the atmosphere, the melodic refrain, the concept, the rhythm, and the setting for the play.

The play is set inside the song. When I was approaching this work, my first question was: where is it set? I considered familiar worldly settings, but then decided on an otherworldly one. Jah is the sole character, and they are speaking from inside a dub song that is speeding through the universe. My next question was: what does the interior of a song look like?

In 2015 I briefly visited Kaieteur National Park in Guyana, South America, the country of my maternal family. The rainforest was the most lush, glorious, and mighty place I have ever been. I decided that the interior of the song had to be a rainforest in full efflorescence: steaming, dripping with green, blooming, sprawling, alive with movement and sound.

Jah is at the centre and is at once confident and thoughtful. They are comfortable in their environment. They move easily between narration and a more internal reflection. In the same way, their physical movement in space shifts between a looser, more fluid groove and a kind of thoughtful pacing. Movement is very important to this character, and not just speech. The opportunity for movement is in the moments of repetition and hesitation in the overall dialogue. The groove is slow and deep, rootsy, but at the same time dreamlike. Dub.

ABOUT THE PLAYWRIGHT

Kaie Kellough is a poet, fiction writer, and sound performer. He has written for small and large musical ensembles and has performed internationally. His most recent book of poetry, *Magnetic Equator* (McClelland and Stewart, 2019) won the 2020 Griffin Poetry Prize. His latest work is the short story collection *Dominoes at the Crossroads* (Véhicule Press, 2020).

ARTIST NOTE

Within the Afrofuturist kaleidoscopic rainforest of a dub tune we meet Jah, travelling inside an everlasting song. A question lingers on the rhythm: Do I return—to the incomplete, to rage, to revolution—or do I rub-a-dub into eternity?

Writer Kaie Kellough took inspiration from the track "Every Dub Shall Scrub" by Scientist, a Babalawo of dub music who trained under the genre's founder, King Tubby. Dub embodies a cultural revolution in Jamaica, which reverberated throughout the world, transforming the musical recording process via sonic fragmentation and radical technological experimentation in studio. This new Black soundscape conjured living musical universes through community sound systems, which transported African descendants beyond neo-colonialism to Black utopias soaked in the sweat of dancehall and decolonization.

It is in one of these universes that we encounter Jah, who invites us to query our own relationship to coloniality, political action, and personal accountability. Jah sings a dub reinterpretation of the original Philippians 2:10-11 Bible verse—"Every knee shall bow / And every tongue confess / On the day / When Jah shall come"—as a warning, an incantation, an invocation, and a proclamation. Jah, or Jah Jah, is the name of God in Rastafari—the anti-colonial socio-religious movement that emerged in Jamaica in the late 1930s. The story's central character, Jah, journeys toward their Godself, being the very transformation that they seek.

In the process of directing the piece, certain questions arose: How do we move toward our Godself as agents of change in the current global political climate? How can we transform rage, make revolution, and achieve completeness? How will we embody ancient African rhythms transmuted across time—becoming dub—as a space of peace?

Jah in the Ever-Expanding Song does not offer answers; instead it reminds us that we—like Jah, like dub—can choose to be transcendent, transformational, and transgressive in the face of ongoing neo-colonial atrocities.

—d'bi.young anitafrika, Director

CHARACTER

Jah: A Black university student in their early twenties.

ATTIRE

Jah is dressed in loose white cotton or linen pants or "skirt" and long top, in the style of a *kurta*. Barefoot, no jewellery or other accessories.

SOUND

Sound is electronic, rises and falls in volume, and alludes to a natural setting.

Some ambient sound is always on. Sometimes sparse, sometimes increasing in density.

LIGHTS

Darkness.

Dim, wide spotlight.

Bright, wide spotlight that undergoes slow, subtle shifts in colour as the work progresses.

Exterior. A rainforest at dawn.

JAH stands and stares upward, then sings.

JAH: "Every knee shall bow
And every tongue confess
On the day
When Jah shall come."

JAH pauses as if preparing themselves for a disclosure. They spread their arms to designate their surroundings and they walk in a broad circle.

Every leaf reminds me of someone.
Every flower blooms a name. The bustle
of fronds unfurling in the shade
recalls my city. The soft humidity here,
the way everything breathes together
recalls the Black Student Network at my university.

JAH pauses and slowly, warily, looks up and to the side. Bluish lights.

A blue macaw observes me from that branch.
Now it blinks, smirks
like an irked conscience, sends
worry shivering through me.
Its eyes fix on mine. It knows the question that curls my tongue:

JAH raises their voice, addresses the macaw, and starts to move slowly and fluidly as if negotiating a path among plants and branches.

What if I steer this song home? What—
the macaw
looks like a cluster of hyacinths,
now like a bird.
Its inverted grin
distorts my name:

> *JAH shouts out, and lets their voice slowly fade down into a laugh, then continues moving fluidly as if among overhanging and underlying foliage.*

J- J- J- J- JJJAAAAAAAAAAAAAAAAAAAAAA-
AAAAAAHHHHHHHHHHHHHHH- Ha

I think
back through worry,
through wonder I think
back to Earth. My worry
keeps the stars burning.

My worry
defies gravity, the planets
worry their ancient suns.

I remember my orbits:
my mother
my father, my brother
my partner, my studies, my act—

my politics, my burning
to transform history from a story
of conquest to a story
that returns the grand narrative
to a simple rhythm
undulating through time—

to me.

JAH pauses, sings to themselves, again at a measured volume louder than the first time, loud enough to transfix listeners, and then easily returns to speech.

"Every knee shall bow
And every tongue confess
On the day
When Jah shall come."

Should I return home?
Why?
Here,
released from doubt,
free of need,
the world seems so—
strange.

I remember the repeated
police interventions that led to the deaths of people just like me,
the botched arrests, the profiling—
a prelude to violation, the clips
of assaults in our newsfeeds
fed a malignancy inside of us.
I remember the city's concrete
trampled by demonstrators' feet.

Here, JAH's movement becomes less fluid and more staggered. They exclaim.

An explosion of—

Exterior. A city during the day.

JAH lowers their voice and articulates sharply.

Justice.

That might have healed us.

JAH goes quiet, as if stifling anger, and continues in a more measured tone while moving again, haltingly, with effort, as if something were holding them back.

Our meetings seemed to give off sparks.
We thought they would ignite the campus.

We tended our anger
like a resource: we channelled it
into ruin and renewal.

Some of us believed
our anger would consume
history as it was written
against us.   Some of us,
confused by ambition, believed
success a cure for collective—

JAH paces stiffly, but in a widening arc, perplexed, as if searching for the next word.

Ambush.   A reimagining.
We decided
to ambush a colonial statue.
It was a time
of the over-
throw of sorrow, of dashing to pieces
the past, of piercing
into a new verity.

Defiance
was our duty.

Deliverance into freedom
proved our being.

If we yanked down the past, would we vanish?
Or would we be realized?

Would we be wrestled to the pavement?
Arrested?

We fought
fear.

JAH's pacing suddenly becomes quicker, less jerky, more assured.

In our meetings we listened to—

JAH speak-sings the names of songs in a rhythmic way, pausing after each one and "discovering" each one anew.

"Downpressor Man"

"Talkin' 'Bout a Revolution"

"Mississippi Goddam"

"Soul Rebel"

Songs in whose
sorrow time trembles.

A single riff
can reverberate through a life.

What good is music if you can't ride
inside its lushness

if it can't provide escape
from the trouble of the world?

That's why we made
music against death

so that each of our children
could fly through reefs of starlight and time.

When I escape my skeleton,
what note
will I light on?

JAH allows the question to linger.

I once saw inside the Earth.
I saw a relentless clock. As it ticked,

rubber bullets flew into crowds.
Flames nibbled at continents. Oil slicked the oceans.

JAH pauses, chuckles to themself, then brushes their shoulders off and grooves subtly to a melody only they can hear. As they groove they move in a still-widening arc.

I believed
my hustle

was the struggle,
that my success

was your liberation—
the truth   was lonelier

my success was mine   alone.
"Mine alone,"

my house, my family, my money,
it's a . . .

(singing) "It's a sh-a-a-ame . . . "

It's a sham.
It's the problem. It's—

JAH appears startled, cuts off the previous thought, and interrupts themselves sharply with the next.

Black hands were grabbing memorials to Civil War generals and pulling them into reality.
Bronze prime ministers were roped and jerked from their pedestals.
"RHODES MUST FALL" echoed across hemispheres.
University endowments founded by enslavers were chanted down on Twitter.

We decided to plant an exclamation point in the radical earth,
to deface a statue and post the footage online.

The following statements grow in intensity as they accumulate. JAH*'s gestures become increasingly grand and expressive.*

It was a statue of Christopher Columbus
of Ronald A. Macdonald
of Hernán Cortés
of the prime minister in blackface
of James Bond with a giant white erection
of a Catholic priest with flames in his eyes
of Cecil Rhodes strangling a dollar bill
of a police officer with his knee on the world's neck.

Exterior. A city at night.

Pause. JAH *seethes in silence a moment. Then* JAH*'s voice lowers slightly. At this point, the arc of* JAH*'s movement on the stage is the widest.*

I climbed the statue.

My allies shone flashlights upward and filmed my ascent. Some broadcast it online. At first the climb was tentative, but I got used to the cool metal under my hands.

When I reached its head, lit by a streetlamp, swarmed by mosquitoes that suddenly became tiny insectile stars, I planned to pour red paint over it.

I concede, the red paint was dramatic. It would ensnare everyone in a wet web of guilt. The red paint suddenly seemed—at that height—aesthetically loud.

The monument shivered.
It wasn't solid.

JAH repeats that single phrase, louder, as if in surprise.

It wasn't solid.
I thought it was iron,

but it might have been copper, or some softer metal,
or maybe just cheap and impermanent,

maybe just dreams and hubris.
I think it was tacky dreams and cheaper hubris.

I reached the shoulders. I grasped the neck.
A cheer rose from the ground.

I felt
like a conqueror.

I hesitated—then—
lifted the paint tin over its head.

"We—we
are shaping a new—"

The statue crumpled and pitched forward.
I clung to the neck with one hand.

My other hand grasped at mosquitoes.
The paint spilled.

Someone in the crowd shouted out my name as the statue fell in slow motion:

JAH shouts/sings the word, drawing out the syllable like a note:

JJJJJJJJJJJJJJJJJJJJJJJJJJJJJJJJAAAAAAAAAAAAAAAAAAAAAAAAAAAAA-
AAAAAAAAAAAAAAAAAAAAAAAAAAAAHHHHHHHHHHHH

JAH goes still for a second as the shout lingers in the air, looks after it as if following it somewhere.

Jah.
That one syllable stretched into a song.
As I tumbled toward the earth, I realized it was a dub tune my parents used to play.
I fell, but I never struck—

JAH stands still with hands up in the air, as if falling.

The statue's head rolled into a pool of paint.
Its red face turned upward. Its mouth grinned and opened,
but it was no longer a mouth,

it was a giant hibiscus flower in full bloom.
I plunged through its centre. Dub
honeyed the air around me.

Exterior. A rainforest at dawn.

JAH stands still and looks, but this time they look at the audience as if observing small figures from a height. Lights acquire a bluish tint as JAH observes.

A blue macaw was standing on a branch.
It fixed me with one supercilious eye:

"Do you want my opinion?"

"On Earth you're probably a giant red pancake."

"You suffered. Welcome to your eternal song."

A question appeared in my thoughts, the only possible question.

"You want to go back? You can . . . in theory." The macaw flew up into the canopy. I heard a screech:

JJJJJJJJJAAAAAAAAAAAAAAAAAAAAAAAAAAHHHHHHHHH

JAH dances and struts about as if enamoured of their surroundings, totally at home and pleased.

I am here, inside the mobile architecture of a song.

JAH hums the "every knee shall bow" refrain slowly, but without pronouncing the words, just humming the melody before speaking.

Remember:
I toppled a monument.

JAH grooves to themselves quietly for a moment, then straightens and looks directly at the audience.

Remember,
my name was Jah.
I lived. I remain.

JAH continues looking directly at the audience, singing:

"Every knee shall bow
and every tongue confess
on the day
when Jah shall come."

BEYERE

SHAUNTAY GRANT

Performer: Natasha “Courage” Bacchus
Director: Lisa Karen Cox

To Tyshana and Ajahni

ACKNOWLEDGEMENTS

My thanks to a wonderful creative team: director Lisa Karen Cox; actor/ASL Coach Natasha "Courage" Bacchus; dramaturge, ASL Interpreters Marcia Martins and Denica C. Brown; Artistic ASL Consultant Dr. Jenelle Rouse. Many thanks also to Mumbi Tindyebwa Otu and the team at Obsidian Theatre Company for the opportunity to be part of this exciting series.

ABOUT THE PLAYWRIGHT

Shauntay Grant is a playwright, poet, interdisciplinary artist, and children's author who lives and works in Kjipuktuk, Mi'kma'ki (Halifax, Nova Scotia). She is Associate Professor of Creative Writing at Dalhousie University and a member of the Royal Society of Canada's College of New Scholars, Artists, and Scientists. A former poet laureate for the City of Halifax, she "creates artworks that are engaging and accessible, but also challenging, rigorous, and informed by deep research" (The Royal Society of Canada). Her stage plays include *The Bridge*, winner of four Robert Merritt Awards. She is the editor of *From The Ashes: Six Solo Plays*, which collects groundbreaking solo plays from the past decade by Black Canadian women and womxn, and she is the author of nine books for children, including *Africville*, winner of the Marilyn Baillie Picture Book Award and a finalist for the Governor General's Literary Award. Grant is a founding member of the interdisciplinary arts group Erasure Art Collective, and she has exhibited at galleries and museums across the country.

ARTIST NOTE

Hello! My name is Courage. My real name is Natasha Bacchus, and the character that I'm playing is Aodri. It was an honour to rehearse with director Lisa Cox and be part of the production of *21 Black Futures.*

I've never had the chance to experience working and rehearsing with a Black theatre company. I kept reading this script by Shauntay Grant and became fascinated. The use of African American vernacular in the script was challenging to translate into ASL, though I learned a lot, and the story reminds me of getting back to the connection of where I'm from.

My family is from Guyana, historically part of the African diaspora. *21 Black Futures* has helped me become more immersed in African art and poetry and uses of language. It's made me research! I want to thank you for being part of this production. Thank you for having me!

—Natasha "Courage" Bacchus, Actor

CHARACTER

Aodri

Interior. One-room apartment—6:00 p.m.

AODRI *cooks fish at home hours after being diagnosed with a terminal illness. She speaks to her daughter Bena—using sign language and devised gestures—while tending to the fish.*

AODRI: Yes. That's it. Now turn your head to that side. No, the other side. Chin up. Not too much. Okay. Now, relax the other shoulder and sink into that hip.

Beat.

It should feel like one side of you is tired and the other is geared up, ready to move.

AODRI *embodies* Ch.

That's it. This is *Ch.*

AODRI *thrusts her hands forward for emphasis as she says the word.*

Now turn to me.

Beat.

Put your hands here, and here.

AODRI *places one hand on her heart, the other on her womb.*

Breathe.

Beat.

Deep, Bena. Till you can feel your breath press into your hands. You feel that? This is *Aoma*.

AODRI *watches Bena embody Aoma; she nods in approval.*

Aoma.

Beat.

Now lift your back and let go your neck. Forward. Eyes up. Soft, but strong.

AODRI *embodies* Beyere *with Bena.*

Yes. That's it. This is *Beyere*.

AODRI *reacts; Bena moves to console her.*

I'm good. You ready to eat?

Beat.

Here. Taste this.

AODRI *hands Bena a small plate with fish.*

Fish. Can you believe it? I got it from Ms. Esther on the way home. She swore to me up and down that it's salmon.

Beat.

The size is off.

AODRI *inspects the fish.*

Who knows. Could be salmon. Everything's off these days.

Beat.

Go ahead. Take a bite.

Beat.

I know, too much pepper, right? Drink this.

Beat.

I don't know how she did it, but somehow Ms. Esther managed to grow scotch bonnet. A whole bunch of them. Like eight or nine. Can you believe it? I wonder where she got the seeds. I begged her a small piece to go with the fish.

AODRI takes a bite of her fish and makes a face.

Forgot how strong it was, though. Been years since we had anything like it. Anything shipped in from overseas, I mean. It was worth it, right?

AODRI takes another bite. Bena simulates choking; AODRI laughs.

(chewing) All right. You right. Tastes like shit.

Beat.

Somethin' ain't right about it—it's not just the pepper. But eat it anyways. It ain't necessarily *bad*; if it was you'd be sick by now. So go on. Eat it. What don't kill you only make you tough. Remember I said that. Now, *Ch*.

Beat.

Eat.

AODRI watches her daughter eat and, after a short while, gets Bena's attention.

I ever tell you where our language comes from? It was long ago. Before we were scattered. Who knows, the two of us, we might be the last of the *Ebanu* people.

Beat.

Anyway, after they took us . . . chained us together in floating caskets, so many never made it . . . dropped us on an island to cut cane bareback, all day under a breaking sun . . . we soon grew tired and ran away to the dark, inner forest.

Beat.

Two-hundred years we lived there, black and untouched. We were hunters and gatherers, roaming jade forests for ripe fruit and wild game. We made big, buff drums from wood and whisk . . . warmed them by massive fires, brighter than even the brightest moons . . . and we danced!

Beat.

Things are rarely lost, Bena. Only stored somewhere.

AODRI *goes back to teaching Bena the gestured words.*

This is *Ayeshwa*. See? You are doing it and I haven't even shown you. This is what I need you to remember, the way the language feels inside your bones. Don't worry that we don't hear. We shape our words with our hands, hips, shoulders . . . remember that, Bena. This language is inside you already. Put your hands here. And here.

AODRI *places one hand on her heart, the other on her womb. Bena follows, and* AODRI *nods in approval.*

Yes. *Aoma.*

Beat.

I have something for you.

AODRI *retrieves a small green plant potted inside a simple flowerpot. Bena asks "Ms. Esther?"*

Yes. Ms. Esther. That woman was sure to take all my credit today.

Beat.

This is . . .

AODRI studies the plant.

You know what? I don't know what it is. I forgot to ask. But you know what it reminds me of? See this colour right here?

Beat.

Mama used to tell me how, in the old days, before white people came to *Ebanuland* and we stopped . . . sharing the language . . . dancing *Imaye* . . . centring the ancestors in our prayers. Way back then, when an elder died they weren't . . . put in a box to rot under a wooden cross, or a printed stone. When you died you were wrapped, in a simple shroud. And if you were a woman, you wore a string of forest pearls—tiny pink beads strung into a necklace or a bracelet, the kind that only comes from the *Bekara* tree. And then, once you were put in the soil, covered with the same earth that held you from when you was a child, a bush was planted right above your heart. Mom always said it was so your soul would keep beating, right along with the rhythms of the earth. So that when you turn to ash and dust you become part of what's living.

Beat.

So that you won't never die.

Beat.

Here.

AODRI hands the plant to Bena. Bena reacts, refuses to accept the plant.

Take it, Bena. Please. It's okay.

Bena still refuses the plant.

It's just life. One minute we here, the next we not. But the words, the stories, the dance, and the people they come from . . .

Beat.

They will all go, Bena, but somehow, never leave. Remember that.

AODRI *offers the plant to Bena again. Bena hesitates, then takes the plant, puts it down.*

Aoma.

Bena embodies Aoma.

Yes. It means "Mother." Now Ch.

Bena embodies Ch.

Faith. Purpose. Determination and strength. All wrapped in one.

Bena embodies Beyere.

Beyere. Meaning "hope."

Beat.

A name. For when you have a daughter.

Bena embodies Ayeshwa.

Ayeshwa. Good, Bena. This is home.

MADNESS WITH ROCKS

PEACE AKINTADE-OLUWAGBEYE

Performer: Dion Johnstone
Director: Jamie Robinson

I dedicate this play to my mother, Titilayo Akintade, who would sit my sibling and I in our one-bedroom apartment, and under blankets, tell us stories of tortoises and foxes. Those folklore gave me hope. Through stories, through my mother, I find hope.

ABOUT THE PLAYWRIGHT

Peace Akintade-Oluwagbeye is an African Canadian interdisciplinary poet, public speaker, chorus-poem playwright, and thespian residing in Saskatoon, Saskatchewan. Organically from Yorubaland, Nigeria, Peace explores the intersectionality of the artist community from an explorer's perspective, dipping her honey-stained fingers into poetry, dance, performance art, critical research, and the theatre world. Her poems express her undying love for ironic justice, motivational banter, the dimmed light of Africa's internal dilemma, and the trouble of cultural barriers. She is the recipient of the 2022 SaskArts RBC Emerging Artist Award and the 2023 Queen's Platinum Jubilee Medal. She was the 2020/2021 Saskatchewan Youth Poet Laurate, the 2022/2023 READSaskatoon Poet Laurate, and the 2023 Poet-in-Residence with the Remai Modern Gallery for their Here and Now: Live Arts Initiative.

ARTIST NOTE

When the damage has been done, how do we heal? What does it mean to truly forgive? The history of Africa has been told best through oral storytelling, its lessons passed down through generations. In Peace Akintade's allegorical tale, a warrior struggles to rediscover his lost tribe and his heritage to heal after his oppressor's harm to Mother Africa. Today, we must all heal from our immediate past and strive for harmony in the future—without blame, shame, or amnesia. Rather than madly demanding change from solid rocks, we must see these formations for what they really are: grains of sand that can be nurtured in the palm of our hand. It is from this peaceful place that you, the audience, are invited—with the click of a button—to hear the warrior's story upon a theatre stage. Mother Africa is by your side and always willing to forgive, if you truly want it.

—Jamie Robinson, Director

CHARACTER

Warrior

ACT ONE: MADNESS WITH ROCKS

Exterior. Wilderness—day.

A rock is placed on the stage. We as the audience meet the WARRIOR *as he wanders around the space.*

The WARRIOR *notices the rock. He is surprised, and searches for more evidence of his tribe's presence. After a fruitless search, he speaks to the rock. Hoping it will listen to his story.*

WARRIOR: Here lies the remains of my tribe.
Blanketed to muffle her curves,
Asleep, stretched on fur skirts;
Named when spring forsook her nerves.

The men leave Africa with oil and gold.
And Africa? She yells of being ruined.
Where were you when once loved?
Where are the cries for violation?

I have no name
I have no title under my tongue
I have been swung by a thin robe of shame.

If a paragraph is better than silence
Do not silence me anymore.
Hear my story, robe-bringers.
Time reminds me every day
That my bruises are not the evidence.
They are instruments for pity,
And a reminder of scorns.

Looking down at the rock, he waits for a response. Silence greets him.

Would Mother Nature still kiss my sunken eyes?
Still ask for my strength?
Each word she swirled into morning soups over and over.
Trapping each sound underneath my tongue.

Speaking more frantically to the empty space.

Mr. Businessman looked at the African
Struggling to remove herself from quicksand.
Ever so slowly reciting scriptures that meant nothing.
Yet the woman wrapped every strand
Of her lover's hair to pull herself up.
Screaming and gasping for a symbol of hope.

And among the vibrant lights of the world,
She finally understands what it means
To prove one's existence.
Explaining why she deserves to fight.
Why she deserves to scream her rights to dry walls.
The African sinks deeper into the quicksand.

She sings for the entertainment of the world.
Do they lend an arm?
Do they know of the scrapes that are caused from praying on her knees?
Do they know of the sons of Karma and the daughters of Circumstance?
We are born without a second look,
And tossed into the quicksand of our colour.

Mother, can I fully cry out in the face of darkness?

They taunt me,
Asking for me to remember dead cultures and forgotten notes.
The silence of destruction
Slow and defeating.

Back to the rock, he collapses next to it.

Again, he waits for the rock to speak, silence meets him.

The cry, the cry of madness
Leave me to rot with knowledge.
Leave me to cry madness
Into the ears of rocks.

How fickle our memories are.
That I cannot decipher the taste of palm wine.
But can experience the drunkenness of lost cultures.

Imagine, sand
Running down my calloused hands.
As it falls, the sand scrapes open wounds.
A forbidden kiss. Morality's kiss.

ACT TWO: CHILDHOOD MEMORIES

Exterior. Wilderness—day.

Speaking into the void, the WARRIOR *relaxes onto the floor next to the rock. He begins to reminisce of his childhood. In the background, a talking-drum begins to play, matching his speed.*

WARRIOR: The sand, my mother, slipping through my soul.
Her voice

Drum beat.

Her voice

Drum beat.

Her advice

Drum beat.

My mother's favourite words were
Memory

Drum beat.

United

Drum beat.

and Nature's Friend.

Drum beat.

Words were so fleeting
We trapped them in music.
My family danced to nothing but drumbeats.
There was a time
When we would sing proverbs
To our Kings and Queens.
Now, we sing our songs for tokens on the streets.
Mr. Businessman calling to hire circus acts
With strange tongues.
Calling for diversity.

Drum beat.

Drum beat.

Drum beat.

The kids circled around the storyteller
Leaning into his every word.
He stood, towering over our minds,
Teaching us odes to nature.
I remember laughing as syrup dripped
Down his chin while he talked.
In between morals hidden in folklore,
He would offer chocolate as a substitute for love.

How would I not remember?
If not for the tattoo inside my ears.

He stands up, as if to mimic the STORYTELLER *from his memory. Awkwardly positions himself in front of the rock, his only audience.*

WARRIOR/STORYTELLER: An ode to nature
And its unrelenting hospitality.
The flow of wheat has always been my lullaby.
Enclosed in its comfort and quiet shame.
The sun keeps calling on us to forgive.
I wonder what that means,
What that looks like.

Is forgiveness like the drop of a penny
Or as silent as the pin.
I wonder how nature describes us:
Dim-witted or vulnerable?
Do they gossip about us?
The murder of crows telling each neighbour secrets.
How did we fall for their tricks?
I wonder whether oceans cry folly at the sailors,
Whether the yowls of the waves are mermaids.
The tides, their playground.
Do they wish us dead or forgive our mistakes?
A rock welcomes the ants to go rest on its stomach:
Is this forgiveness, calmness?

Finishing his imitation of the STORYTELLER, *he stands, still confused.*

WARRIOR: Is forgiveness calmness?
Mother Nature,
Can the stories recited over moonlights and palm wines
Be the remaining existence of my culture?

ACT THREE: MOTHER'S ADVICE

Exterior. Wilderness—day.

Walking around the space, he laments the emptiness, rubbing the words underneath his tongues. Pondering the meaning behind the statement.

WARRIOR: My mother pulled me by the ears
When I mocked the storyteller's lisp at seven.
She told me to always be watchful of vultures,
To always whisper to my hands
And tell them they are powerful.
She told me the secret to life was control.
To control what you say, in turn, what you do.
Fighters will always escape disappointment, she said,
For they have the power of words.

WARRIOR/STORYTELLER: My dear brothers and sisters, take note of this:
My mother told me the tongue can crush the spirit.
Therefore, let your words always be seasoned with grace.
She tells me: your words have influence in the course of history.
Your tongue is the definition of a phoenix's throne.
Mother, did you know others bow on a throne of lies?
Do you know the world has decided to worship vultures,
And sing of violence in a forsaken note?
Tell me that my hands have more meaning,
That they no longer need to shield from my consequences.
Can you hear the children cry havoc on their friends,
And wonder why destruction is so close to speaking?
The tongue holds authority to influence your manifestation.
Therefore, I say, you are with me.
In the stories passed on by storytellers like I.

Finally he addresses the audience, fully confident of his position as the new STORYTELLER.

MADNESS WITH ROCKS

STORYTELLER: Children, when you're finally free from the quicksand,
Admire the powerful swirls and rich colour.
Notice how it never stops for anyone,
How it creates beauty on Earth.
Begin to fall in love with your prisoner.

I am still trying to be human;
Adapting to the growing rules.
To be human, I know
Is to clench to life
To quench the curiosity,
And rediscover
A new meaning to choice.
I choose to love my heritage.
While I am still breathing.
The sun rotates, gleefully unaware of its influence:
Let us be more like the sun,
Unaware of the touches that make legends.
Let the grass wrap their feather gaze on our bruised knee
Healing our past with sweet nothings and
Brighter accession of time.

Begin to speak of power, because you are the last one standing.
Africa remains barren and silent
But our voices shall fill the land.
The fragments of our forgotten culture
Are buds hidden among the sand.
Let us allow the destruction to feed our soul.
One day we will live on, fondness in our heart.
Stories underneath our tongue.

The STORYTELLER *slowly picks up the rock, holds it like a child, and exits with peace.*

End.

WITNESS SHIFT

DONNA-MICHELLE ST. BERNARD

Performer: Uche Ama
Director: Sarah Waisvisz

ACKNOWLEDGEMENTS

I am grateful to the village

for contributing perspective to development of this piece: Keith Barker, Courage Bacchus, Sarah Waisvisz, Uche Ama, Abigail Whitney, Kern Albert, Brenda St. Bernard.

for contributing images and energy to the production: Luke Reece, Peace Akintade, Emerjade Simms, Lovell Adams-Gray, Stephanie Mazunya, Sarah Waisvisz.

for stewarding this incredible feat: Mumbi Tindyebwa Otu, Myekah Payne, Michael Sinclair, Malina Patel, Fatuma Adar.

ABOUT THE PLAYWRIGHT

Donna-Michelle St. Bernard aka Belladonna the Blest is an emcee, playwright, agitator, and practitioner of humanitarian arts. Her main body of work, the 54ology, includes *Cake*, *Sound of the Beast*, *A Man A Fish*, *Salome's Clothes*, *Gas Girls*, *Give It Up*, *The Smell of Horses*, *Bilguisa Speaks Up*, *Diggers*, *Conjugal*, *Hunt/Peck*, and *The First Stone*. Other theatre works include *Reaching For Starlight*, *They Say He Fell*, and *The Final Inquiry*. Libretti include *Forbidden* (Afarin Mansouri/Tapestry Opera) and *Oubliette* (Ivan Barbotin/Tapestry Opera). She is co-editor with Yvette Nolan of the anthology *Refractions: Solo* (2014) and *Refractions: Scenes* (2020) and editor of *Indian Act: Residential School Plays* (2018), all published with Playwrights Canada Press.

ARTIST NOTE

The policing system in North America was born out of—indeed, born in order to support—the structures that upheld slavery and genocide. Since we know this to be true, why do we allow it to persist? Isn't there another way to serve and protect our communities so we can meet the needs of the most vulnerable?

Donna-Michelle St. Bernard's *Witness Shift* challenges us to imagine a future in which calling the cops is not the only option in an emergency; a future in which the aspirations to "Abolish the Police" and "Defund the Police" are allowed to play out. The play offers us a model to explore the steps we need to take to transform our society so each of us can truly be seen in our full humanity and each of us can truly be free.

Witness Shift is dedicated to Regis, Breonna, Abdirahman, and everyone who deserved a different system.

—Sarah Waisvisz, Director

CHARACTER

Witness

Interior. Operator's station—night.

WITNESS sits at their workstation facing a screen. They are connected to a trainee operator and various emergency services. They begin by adjusting the workstation from the prior user's shift—rearview mirror adjusting kinda stuff. Details of the Requestor may appear onscreen, or an "ENGAGED" indicator, as needed.

WITNESS: Got your water? Notepad? Cue up the resource list. I'm muting your mic.

WITNESS shuffles papers or screens or whatev.

First we clear day shift's loose ends. Let's see. Two pantry requests—we can get those onto the next truck out. The third one requires a transmasc operator. Can you reroute this to team . . . B? That's griss. Decks cleared.

Now, I'll take the first few calls, then we'll see about putting you on. Look at your face. You'll do fine. I've trained over fifty witnesses, some greener than you, and every one of them still in the field. This ain't just a shift, it's a tour of duty. Now, I've been a Witness so long, I basically got eight days till retirement. No, not really. It was a reference. Never mind. Who knows, knows. You don't know.

This guy. You don't know. This guy. Says to me, "Yeah, but does anything ever change? Actually?"

I see change every day, youngblood. You ain't had your eyes open long enough to look, but I see it.

Ping!

Okay, we have about fifteen seconds to scan the file. Requestor has been granted court-ordered access to return to the marital home. Retrieving personal property subsequent to a separation decree. No intervention indicated. Requestor is activating visual contact.

WITNESS engages the microphone.

Sir, please be aware that I have been asked to attend as a witness to this encounter.

Please maintain a distance of three feet, sir. Let's have an uneventful day, friends.

WITNESS watches for a moment, checking off inventory items.

Thank you. Disengage when you are ready.

WITNESS disengages the call.

Oh yes, things have changed. Because I don't remember anyone ever having the audacity to ask such a ridiculous question, straight-faced and bold. I must be getting old or soft, for you to be letting off like this, wasting my time and erasing the tribulations and overcoming of generations. Are you kidding me? Does anything change . . .

Ping!

Mental health distress. Family is requesting a witness to prevent risk of self-harm. Rookie, access the file and identify an available support worker in the area—stat. Make sure they get the brief. I want a chime when they're at the door. Scanning the file. Not our first time out, so no need to go in skittish. There's a note . . . yes. Requesting consent for direct engagement through lifeline device.

WITNESS finds a note in the file, quickly hums tune to self to get it right. Engage signal comes through.

Accepted.

WITNESS raises voice slightly to sing a version of "Rockin' Robin." She listens while singing for any vocalizations from the Requestor. A chime indicates that help has arrived.

Hey friend, there's a support worker at the door. Can they come in?

I can stay if you like. It's your choice. Disengage when you are ready.

WITNESS waits, then disengages the call.

I mean, seriously, change is real. I know it. I see it right now, in this moment. I see it in the way I stayed in place; the way I didn't jump up to thump up your face like when I was younger. When I was bucked up. Relax. Fill your gaps. Sit, listen, learn—and don't churn the pot. Can't sip from a spoon with slots.

Ping!

Intervention request. Originating from personal mobile device. Requestor declines identification. Privacy filters active. Going on screen.

WITNESS listens, nods, signs to a Deaf Requestor using BASL.

[How did you end up at the only hair salon in town that doesn't sign? That's wild. I will transfer you to a dedicated interpreter. Please stand by . . . you're welcome.]

WITNESS disengages the call.

Rookie, can you handle that?

WITNESS shakes their head.

Has anything? Ever?! I say, it must have. Used to be someone your age knew better than to be that wrong that loudly, and surely not in front of anybody. How embarrassing, to even ask that. This frigging guy.

Ping!

Low-priority call. Originating from community call box. Oh no! Missing dog? That's not low priority. Rude. You want to make this call, Rookie? Who can we spare? Sure, we could send cops. Let 'em have one. They're getting dusty. But let's take another look at the file. Is there any chance, any chance at all, that this call could involve human interaction? Right. So instead of cops, we might go with . . . ?

WITNESS waits for an answer.

Animal welfare. Now you're thinking—go with it. And make sure the crossing guards in that area know to keep an eye out.

WITNESS dispatches the call.

Does anything change, he says. I say, what are you doing to make it? You got the strength for a patience game or do you need to see change on the daily to believe in it? Then look.

Ping!

Incoming call from a minor. Auto-record engaged. Going on screen per request.

WITNESS clicks the screen on, then listens intently.

Oh no. Who told you you're ugly? Oh, baby, no. That person's got ugly behaviour, hear me? They said what? I cannot. Listen, can you say prosopagnosia? Me either, hardly. It's a condition some people have, where they can't see faces. Yeah. Like they wouldn't know the difference between you and me, no matter how long they look. Doesn't that make you wonder what someone else's eyes might be telling them? Maybe it's nothing to do with how you really look, who you really are. Can you say that word I taught you? Prosopagnosia. Good. Practise it a couple of times.

WITNESS mutes self, listens to Rookie in earpiece.

Yeah, well, that's what-all I came up with. Oh, you got this? All right, go. Send your packet.

WITNESS turns attention back to child. A series of images flash across the screen: beautiful Black people, different ages, skin tones, body types, and aesthetics. The child's image has been slipped into the array.

Does that look ugly to you? How about that? See this radiance? Who's that? Stunning. That's right. Wow is right, baby. You go on and have a big day today.

WITNESS disengages the call. Rests.

And so the student, eh? That's griss. This guy. Does anything change, he says, holding back on a stack of intuition that can't be trained. Ask me, only one thing remains.

Breathe deep, Rookie. I'm going to switch you over to Lead Witness. Look at your face. I'll be here, but you already know how we do. We take care of each other. Begin, now.

WITNESS smiles warmly into the camera and switches over. There may be a screen that indicates that the Witness Shift has passed over to the audience.

End.

SENSITIVITY

LAWRENCE HILL

Performer: Sabryn Rock
Director: Mike Payette

ABOUT THE PLAYWRIGHT

Lawrence Hill is a writer whose novels and works of non-fiction have been widely read in Canada, translated into many languages, and published around the world. He is a professor of creative writing at the University of Guelph, and has served as a mentor to Canadian writers for more than thirty years. Hill is the winner of various awards, including the National Magazine Award for best feature article ("Is Africa's Pain Black America's Burden?"), the Commonwealth Writers' Prize and the Rogers Writers' Trust Fiction Prize for his novel *The Book of Negroes*, and twice has won CBC's Canada Reads. Hill co-wrote the adaptation for the six-part television miniseries *The Book of Negroes*, which won eleven Canadian Screen Awards. His volunteer activities include serving as an honorary patron of Crossroads International, whose work in community economic development in sub-Saharan Africa he has actively supported for forty years.

ARTIST NOTE

It's a few years from the present, and Gabriaela Monk misses her GO train to Hamilton. She's just been fired from her long-standing job as the only racial sensitivity trainer at Connect International, one of Canada's leading dating services. The aftermath for Gabriaela is a complex and honest reliving of what led her to this moment, negotiating the wisdom of her deceased mother and the voices that challenge the relevance and value of sensitivity work in these times.

Lawrence Hill weaves a singular narrative about one woman's personal investigation, through humour and questioning, and her quest for hope and to reclaim her dignity. It's a contemporary and deeply resonant piece that asks us to remember who we are and what we believe in when confronted with those who challenge us.

—Mike Payette, Director

CHARACTER

Gabriaela [pronounced Ga-bree-AY-la] Monk: Forty-one, biracial Black woman. Dressed as a professional.

SETTING

Nighttime, at the far end of an isolated platform of a commuter train station. Train tracks lead out into the night: stars and skyline. One bench and a trash can, and, on other side of the set, another bench in the middle of a semicircle of six empty chairs.

TRAIN CONDUCTOR: *(voice-over)* 9:43 p.m. Westbound train to Hamilton. Track nine. Doors closing.

The sound of doors closing. GABRIAELA, *with purse in one hand and briefcase in the other, races onto the set.*

GABRIAELA: Wait. Hold up.

A letter falls out of her pocket. GABRIAELA *stops to pick it up, runs to the end of the platform. The train bells clang.*

Fuck. Fucker! Goddamn train. Can a train be racist? Damn right. It would have waited for a white woman. "Oh, excuse me, I'm coming, if you could wait a moment." "Certainly, Madam, get on board. There you go. Take a seat. Get comfortable."

Well, I'm not comfortable.

GABRIAELA *shouts.*

I'm not comfortable.

The sound of the train fades to quietness. Outside, birds tweet in the darkness. GABRIAELA *opens her purse, blows her nose, walks to a trash can and throws out the tissue.*

LOUDSPEAKER: *(voice-over)* The next westbound train leaves in one hour, at 10:43 p.m.

GABRIAELA *kicks the trash can. Limps away. Stares at the train tracks leading out into the night. Scans the letter. Opens the briefcase, shoves in the letter. Returns to trash can. Hurls her briefcase against it.*

GABRIAELA: "Fired with cause. Disregard for civility."

Are you kidding me? I gave you six years, Connect International.

> *GABRIAELA walks to the bench. Sits. Drums her fingers on the briefcase. Opens it again, examines letter, studies a cheque. Puts it all back.*

Fifty-thousand dollars to make me go away. Because I make them uncomfortable.

> *GABRIAELA rubs the briefcase.*

Connect International. The country's most successful dating app for singles over thirty-five.

Some good it's done me.

> *GABRIAELA stands. Walks to edge of platform.*

Six years of commuting from Hamilton. Six-day weeks and Sunday emails. Six years of making my lunch, no lettuce or peanut butter because we can't have a Black professional with food stuck in her teeth, eating at my desk, and pretending to care at the water cooler.

"Joe, it's so sad that your Golden Doodle Poodle Schmoodle passed away."

"Charlotte, I hear you. Blonde hair, straight as a knife. All that humidity with five days of rain messes with your blowout."

> *GABRIAELA walks along the train tracks. She opens her purse, removes tissues, wipes the bench, and sits down again.*

Mama said never sit on public benches.

> *GABRIAELA transitions into her mother's voice.*

Benches, Mama said, were not for upwardly mobile Coloured people. Benches were for transients.

(as her mother) Mere threads of clothing separate a park bench and the last occupant's rectum!

(replying to her mother) Mama, that's wack as hell. Folks need benches. And we don't say upwardly mobile anymore. We don't say Coloured either.

(as her mother) I started out as Coloured a long time ago. What is this with Black? Is Black the colour of my skin? Do we say red or yellow? No, we do not. We do say white, that's true. But that's their own fault for, well, four hundred years of acting like white folks.

My dear Gabriaela, if I can't say Coloured, you can't say Black. What about your father?

(to her mother) White as bird shit on a fence post, but a good man.

> GABRIAELA *sighs heavily.*

Mama. There was no need for you to rush off and join Papa so soon.

> *She walks to the far edge of the platform. Listens to the birds. She looks up, past the skyline of high-rises, to the dark skies.*

I like to think that the souls of Black folks inhabit those stars. When it's my turn to go, somebody please transport me to one of those stars. Sit my tired butt down. I wonder if anybody, on any one of those stars, has ever, ever, ever been asked to lead a racial sensitivity training seminar.

> *She snorts.*

Sensitivity trainers are banished to the furthest stars. Can't have folks like us blacking up the Milky Way!

(as her mother) Big promotion, six-figure salary, but don't do it, daughter. Avoid sensitivity training like the plague. Coloured woman tells white folks the truth about themselves, and you know what? White folks don't appreciate it one bit.

> GABRIAELA *walks to the bench and sits. She retrieves the cheque, studies it, and shoves it back into the briefcase.*

"Fired with cause." Hmmph.

> GABRIAELA *walks to the speaking bench in the middle of the semicircle of chairs. She prepares to address the imaginary people seated before her. Clears her throat.*

Hello, everyone. I am Gabriaela Monk, director of equity and diversity. We're here to talk about racial sensitivity, and what that means.

> GABRIAELA *squares her shoulders.*

We at Connect International want this to be a safe space. A trusting space.

Who would like to go first?

> GABRIAELA *swings out from behind the bench, and sits in the first chair on her right. She stands, puffs out her chest, and plants her feet flat and wide.*

(as Hector) Hector. Ten years at Connect. I work in IT. You know how I got this job? Merit. Merit, and work ethic. I've got no problem with people, as long as they have no problem with me. Do your job and don't be an asshole. Sensitivity? Some things can't be taught.

> GABRIAELA *walks to the first chair on her left, sits briefly in it, then stands.*

(as Petra) I am Petra. My parents came as refugees from Czechoslovakia, you know. I grew up on Hallam Street. In the winter, we would turn on the oven, open the door, you know, and hold our hands close to the element. I am a single mom and make twenty-eight thousand dollars a year. I don't need sensitivity, you know. I need a raise.

> GABRIAELA *returns to stand behind the speaking bench. She holds up a finger.*

Petra . . . Hector, I hear you but wait . . . wait . . . could you consider this fact? We have five thousand employees. Eight of us are Black or Indigenous. Eight.

Now, while we think about that, let's let everyone introduce themselves.

> *GABRIAELA leaves the speaking bench. She walks back to the bench at the end of the station platform. She opens a lunch bag, pulls out an ice pack, and retrieves a sandwich. She takes a bite and chews slowly.*

> *GABRIAELA reaches back into her briefcase and pulls out the letter. Unfolds it.*

"Fired with cause . . . failed to maintain control."

What am I? Dog walker with leash?

Never been fired before. Never failed a course.

> *GABRIAELA approaches the speaking bench. She sits in Petra's chair, then stands.*

(as Petra) Excuse me? I don't mean to be offensive, you know, but why are you called Gabriaela? What's wrong with Gabriella? Why do Black girls go with weird names?

> *GABRIAELA returns to the bench.*

(to Petra) Nothing weird about it. I happen to like my name. It's the name my mother gave me. The name she chose for me. I was not invited into the conversation.

> *GABRIAELA turns and steps away from the bench.*

Nearly lost it there.

But so far, so good. I was on my way to a tick. A tick in the box noting that the training unfolded without incident.

I wish.

> *GABRIAELA turns back to the speaking bench, and looks at a chair to her right. Goes to sit in it. Stands quickly.*

(as Monica) I'm Monica. I spoke at the company picnic, Gabriaela, but that seems to have eluded you.

Anyway, my parents came from the Bahamas. University educated, I'll have you know. I've never experienced racism. If you're having a problem, maybe you brought it upon yourself.

And by the way. I applied for your job, Gabriaela. When I didn't get it, I moved over to Human Resources. Much better. I have two graduate degrees, which you do not. See, I did my research. I know all about you. I know that your father was white. And a janitor.

(to Monica) You don't know a thing about me.

GABRIAELA *holds up her hands.*

Let's all take a breath. I suggest a visualization exercise. Could I ask all of you to close your eyes for a moment?

GABRIAELA *returns to sit in a chair, then stands.*

(as Petra) Closing our eyes is childish. Monica has a point, you know. Being half-Black didn't hurt you. You got the job, didn't you?

GABRIAELA *goes to another chair, sits, then stands.*

(as Hector) They made me come here, but I've got work to do. Can we just get to our jobs and stop competing in the sensitivity Olympics?

GABRIAELA *goes to another chair, sits, then stands.*

(as Monica) Listen up, Gabriaela. I know your mother was Black, and a domestic . . . but you're light as day in your cushy job.

GABRIAELA *holds both arms up over the bench.*

(to Monica) Monica, can you please stop?

(as Monica) Half and half.

(to Monica) I am not half of anything.

Half of anything!

I've been Black been since I walked into a store at the age of six and got called you know what.

I was going to tell you about that.

I was going to appeal to your better angels. But they have deserted you. You've got no more heart than dried out corncobs.

You've got to be the most selfish, close-minded people I have met in the company . . . and that's going some distance.

I'm done here. When the Good Lord finishes with you, I hope She sends you straight to hell.

So go, go now, that's right, get out.

> GABRIAELA *walks back to the edge of the train platform. She howls into the night:*

Fuuuck.

> GABRIAELA *sits on the bench.*

No matter how folks act, Mama said, you can't let your guard down. When trouble comes, Mama said, be like steam over a pot. Slip up and slide away.

> GABRIAELA *opens the letter from her employer.*

"If you accept this settlement, you rule out any litigation. You have until 5:00 p.m. on January 25, 2025, to cash the cheque. After that, it shall be rendered null and void."

Mama. Why did I ever take that job? I tried so hard. Six years of feeling responsible for how folks think.

GABRIAELA laughs.

Sign me up for accounting.

Numbers do not talk back. Numbers are in no need of sensitivity.

Sound of an oncoming train, with bells clanging.

LOUDSPEAKER: 10:43 p.m. westbound train to Hamilton. Arriving on track nine.

GABRIAELA: Fire my ass because I lost it on fools? I deserve better. Better.

GABRIAELA rips up the cheque and tosses it down onto the train tracks. It swirls and blows away in the wind.

Free at last. Free at last. Thank God Almighty, I am free at last.

SEASON 2

Season 2 of *21 Black Futures* was produced by Obsidian Theatre Company and CBC Arts, and was first aired on CBC Gem on February 19, 2021.

Special by Keshia Cheesman

Umoja Corp by Jacob Sampson

Notice by Luke Reece

Blackberries by Miali-Elise Coley-Sudlovenick

Emmett by Syrus Marcus Ware

Georgeena by Djanet Sears

Rebirth of the Afronauts by Motion

SPECIAL

KESHIA CHEESMAN

Performer: Avery Grant
Director: Jay Northcott

To the Black girls who feel invisible yet hypervisible at the same time. To the Black girls who feel like they don't belong in any space they navigate. You are enough. You are special.

ABOUT THE PLAYWRIGHT

Keshia Cheesman is a Caribbean Canadian theatre artist based in Mohkinstsis (Calgary, AB). She is as an actor/performer, playwright, deviser, and arts educator, and is known for her play *The F Word*, co-created and performed with Bianca Miranda. She has worked with notable Calgary theatre companies such as The Shakespeare Company, Chromatic Theatre, Swallow-a-Bicycle Theatre, One Yellow Rabbit, Handsome Alice Theatre, Downstage, Alberta Theatre Projects, and Theatre Calgary. Keshia is passionate about creating art rooted in the truth of humanity and told by diverse and marginalized communities, as well as uplifting children and youth through the power of the arts.

ARTIST NOTE

I always wanted to be different. My family are all electricians; I became an artist. Kids in school wanted to play dodge ball; I would meditate (incorrectly) in a corner at recess. That was my identity for a long time: the exact opposite of everyone else.

This is why I connected to Keshia's piece, *Special*. It explores what it means to be different and how identity is a state of mind. It tells the story of an eight-year-old girl trying to find the meaning of life while also struggling to understand the complexity of self. In this play we see how this battle is within all of us, and experience the vulnerability of asking for a sign to tell us, "Am I doing the right thing?"

There has been a shift in Western culture. We have become a melting pot, where access to everyone and everything is more available than ever before.

You can't be different because someone is already doing what you're doing—and probably doing it better than you on TikTok. So what makes you special? That is the question Zari is looking to answer. Isn't it what we are all looking for?

—Jay Northcott, Director

CHARACTER

Zari: eight, dark skin, coarse hair. Very bold and energetic.

2045. Nighttime in ZARI*'s new, small bedroom.*

She is getting ready for bed, finishing her nighttime routine. Her mama just taught her how to moisturize her hair and oil her scalp before bed, and she is doing exactly what she learned.

Mama calls her from another room.

ZARI: YES, MAMA?

Beat.

YES, MAMA! I'm doing it now.

Beat.

YES, MAMA. I will put on my bonnet. GOOD NIGHT!

ZARI *kneels beside her bed to pray.*

Dear God, it's me, Zari. I bet you didn't recognize me from my new room, huh? I know. It's. So. Small. But Mama said I have to be grateful to even have my own room. We had to move in with Grandma because Mama couldn't afford our house anymore since Daddy . . . y'know . . . is with you now. Thanks for taking good care of him. Oh, and can you tell him I've been making my bed every day? He'd like to hear that.

Sorry I haven't talked to you in a while. I started at my new school this week and everyone's nice I guess but . . . I'm having a crisis. Because, okay, so, I thought for my first day of school I'd get Mama to put my hair in twists cuz I know that looks super cute, and at my old school, the one time I did it, all the other kids were super, super jealous cuz they'd say, "Wow! It's so pretty! I wish I could get my hair to look like yours because you look like those super cool famous girls." And I agree. Cuz it makes me look really pretty. Like, really, really pretty. But when I came to my new school, so many other girls had twists too! No one said my hair was pretty or told me they were jealous cuz everyone kinda has the same hair, so we all look like the famous girls. And at recess, I wanted to show everyone the new dance I learned but then a bunch of other kids were doing dances too! And they were really good at it . . . even better than me. And I'm usually the best. Oh, and at lunch, everyone I ate with had rice. Rice!

Some people even had fried fish with their rice like me! Mine looked way yummier than theirs. But still! No one *ever* had rice and fish like me at my old school. And I think this is all because everyone in this town is, well, Black like me. And I asked Mama, "Why is everyone Black like us?" and she said it's because a long time ago before I was born, lots of bad stuff was happening to Black people in Alberta and it wasn't fair, so they all got together and merged two towns, Black Diamond and Turner Valley, to create their own Black town, Diamond Valley. Even Grandma helped! But you know all about this. You're God.

Anyway, I do like that everyone here is kind of the same because I don't feel super different and I actually fit in for once . . . But also, I think I like feeling different. At my old school, the other girls wanted to be like me.

(whispers) And don't tell Mama and Grandma I said that cuz they said I need to "practise humility," but it's true! At my old school I was special. But now I'm just . . . normal.

How can I be special at Diamond Valley Elementary?

Beat.

I know you're busy, but do you think you can help me? Do you have any ideas?

Beat.

If you have a good idea give me a sign. In three . . . two . . . one . . . GO!

Beat.

I said go!

God? Are you even listening to me? I have some big problems here and YOU'RE NOT HELPING!

ZARI's mother yells at her from the other room.

SORRY! I'm just praying, Mama! I'll be quiet!

(quieter) You're not helping. Fine. If you don't wanna help, I guess I'm gonna have to think of ways all. By. My. Self. Amen. Actually, NOT amen cuz I still want you to stay on the line just in case you got an idea.

ZARI aggressively puts on her bonnet.

Wait . . . I've never seen anyone wear their bonnet to school . . . or outside the house. I'm gonna wear my bonnet to school every day! This will make me special! And, and . . . I will even put my hair band on it.

ZARI grabs a hair band and places it on her bonnet.

There! That's kinda cute.

ZARI starts to scratch her arm while brainstorming. She goes to grab some cocoa butter. She examines the cocoa butter, the ashiness on her arm from scratching, and then lets out a dramatic sigh.

Everyone uses cocoa butter, so I guess I'm giving up cocoa butter. If my skin gets itchy, I'm just gonna have to deal with it. Wait. I can't. Grandma said being ashy is a sin. I don't wanna sin. God, I don't want you to hate me! So maybe . . .

ZARI starts applying generous amounts of cocoa butter to her body. She gets carried away and eventually her face and arms are covered in cocoa butter. Comically so.

There we go. Oh yeah. I like this.

Do you know what? I don't wanna be Zari Ilori Mitchell anymore . . . Yuck. That's too plain. I'm gonna be . . . Molly! Molly . . . Mary Mitchell. That sounds famous. Everyone is going to think I'm famous with my new look and name!

Ooo! I'm gonna film this!

ZARI grabs a device, sets it up, and hits record.

Hi, I'm Molly.
Hey, it's Molly.
Moll-ay.
Mall-E.

Hey, girl. Molly here. And welcome to my life. And I'm not like any of you losers. I'm different and I'm special. I bet you wish you could pull off this look. And I don't even eat rice. Who eats rice anymore? Bleh. Fried fish? BLEHHHHH. I eat ummm . . . Pickle sandwiches. Yeah! And I know you're thinking, "Oooo can I have a bite of your special sandwich? I've never had that before." And I'm gonna say, "NO." Because it's for special girls like me and me only.

ZARI pauses the recording.

I'm doing pretty great here, hey, God? Hold on one sec.

ZARI tiptoe-runs to her kitchen to grab a jar of pickles and a bag of bread and comes back to record her sandwich assembly.

So here we have bread, and pickles. Yummy . . . yum . . . pickles . . . And you put the pickles in bread like this!

ZARI finishes assembling her sandwich.

Ta-da!

By the way, I hate dancing. Everyone loves dancing? Not me. I'm specialer so I'm actually a . . . um . . . golf player. Wanna see?

ZARI runs to her closet to grab a ball and a stick. When she grabs the stuff, a letter in an envelope labelled "To Zari" falls on the floor. She does not notice at first and makes a terrible attempt at playing golf.

Ha ha, I'm just rusty. And my hands are just a little . . . um . . . slimy from the cocoa butter. See, if I just try one more time . . .

ZARI whacks the ball hard and it soars across her room, scaring her.

AHH!

Um, I think that's enough golf for today. I'm just gonna have a bite of my super amazing special sandwich.

ZARI shows off her sandwich to the camera and takes a big bite.

Oh wow . . . that's um . . . wow. Strong . . . and just . . .

ZARI rushes to stop recording and then spits out her sandwich.

Ew, ew, ew! GROSS.

(frustrated) I just wanna be special like I used to. And now I can't even be special in a new way without being bad at it.

I wish we never moved to Diamond Valley. Thanks for nothing, God.

ZARI starts to put everything away when she notices the envelope.

"To Zari"? What's this?

ZARI opens the envelope and reads the letter out loud:

"Zari,
You are the most beautiful girl in my eyes,
But nothing is more beautiful than the girl you are inside. You have a heart of gold,
Your personality is bold,
And that's what makes you special,
The essence of your soul.
Love always, Daddy."

Whoa. God! Did you see what just happened? I've never seen that letter before in my life! And it was on my floor and I opened it and it's from Daddy and . . . Wait . . . Did you put that letter there? Did you get Daddy to send that to me? You're sneaky. But I like it.

(aside) God really does work in mysterious ways.

I'm glad I kept you on the line or I'd have to cover my hair at school and be cocoa-butter greasy and play sports and eat pickle sandwiches. Yuck.

ZARI's mother calls from another room.

Yes, Mama. I'm going to bed now.

(to God, quietly) I'm not special because of my hair or my skin or my lunch . . . I'm special because I'm me. Zari Ilori Mitchell. Thanks, Daddy.

Amen.

End.

UMOJA CORP

JACOB SAMPSON

Performer: Pablo Ogunlesi
Director: Leighton Alexander Williams

This is dedicated with deep gratitude to my collective. Those who have taught, guided, and cared for me.

ACKNOWLEDGEMENTS

Umoja Corp was born of the idea of the collective brilliance of Blackness and what is possible when we come together. I am incredibly grateful to Mumbi and the entire Obsidian team, and to director Leighton Alexander Williams and actor Pablo Ogunlesi for their beautiful work in bringing this story to life.

ABOUT THE PLAYWRIGHT

Jacob Sampson grew up in the Annapolis Valley of Nova Scotia and is a descendant of the historic Black community of Beechville. He received his Bachelor of Theatre Studies from Acadia University. Since graduating he has performed in plays such as *The Colour Purple* (Neptune), *Shakespeare in Love* (Neptune), *Chasing Champions* (Ships Company), and *Othello* (Shakespeare by the Sea), and wrote and starred in *Chasing Champions* (Ships Company), which received numerous Nova Scotia Merritt Awards, including Best New Play.

ARTIST NOTE

Charged with fraud and identity theft, Adrian Joy Ellis faces the full wrath of the court system—until Umoja Corp steps in. We join Adrian in isolation as he recounts the steps that led to his imprisonment.

This film tackles themes of isolation. We see its effects on mental health as Adrian spirals downward, making poor choices just to survive. The story is pertinent in this day and age, after COVID-19 lockdowns compounded unemployment, mental health issues, and other societal ills. Stepping into Adrian's shoes is not a difficult task for many, thanks to the events of 2020.

But *Umoja Corp* also explores unity as a major theme—depicting a future in which the Black diaspora steps into our collective power, centring Black women's experiences and perspectives. A love letter to the Black woman, and genuinely beautiful to behold: "We were conquerors when in concordance. We bathed in Gold and birthed the boldest battalions. Wakanda is not a wish. Pharaohs are not fictitious. Our empire is not erased. Black is King. Black has been King. Black will be King, but only if Black joins Queen."

—Leighton Alexander Williams, Director

CHARACTER

Adrian: non-gender specific. Black. Nineteen.

The setting is dark and quiet.

The Umoja chime plays.

We hear the voice of "THE PROSECUTION" cut through the darkness.

THE PROSECUTION: We are here as representatives of the people. We are here to pursue the conviction and prosecution of one Adrian Joy Ellis. Due to the criminal past of the defendant we will push for the harshest sentence allowable by the courts.

Silence.

The voice of THE PROSECUTION is heard again.

We will push for the harshest sentence allowable by the courts.

Lights up.

We are in an intake room. Think any generic waiting room.

We see ADRIAN, nineteen, Black, well dressed (unspecified gender). ADRIAN's eyes are bright and piercing. ADRIAN's posture is one of defiance and looks as though ADRIAN would be unmovable. ADRIAN has a quick cadence, a sharp wit. ADRIAN uses humour and rants to get a point across. We now hear the voice of THE PROSECUTION again and realize it is ADRIAN putting on an imitation. Through the play ADRIAN will transition and imitate characters from the story. This is all meant to happen in front of the audience.

ADRIAN: *(in the voice of THE PROSECUTION)* "The harshest sentence allowable by the courts."

Pause.

That's when my mind woke. That's when I realized that the shit storm I was in wasn't something that I could hunker down and weather through. It had the ability to uproot everything that had become my life and send me to jail. Real jail.

Sound of a jail cell slamming shut.

Pause.

(with grave seriousness) You ever see the inside of a jail?

ADRIAN *speaks directly to the audience. I mean directly through the screen to the individuals watching.*

You. I mean you behind the screen watching me right now. I see you.

There is a very deliberate pause here. The time can be specified by the director and the actor, but the intention is to make the audience know there is no fourth wall. This is happening to them.

And I want to know. Have you ever seen the inside of a jail before? Not the jail you see on broadcasts or in your feeds . . . I mean, real prison?

Giving time for their imaginations to run.

THE PROSECUTION: "We will push for the harshest sentence allowable by the courts."

ADRIAN: Imagine the whole power of the government, being against little ole me. It would be flattering, if it wasn't so utterly terrifying.

A short moment of reflection from ADRIAN.

BUT!!!!

A techno or electronic version of the Canadian national anthem plays in the background.

(faux passion) We are a land of democracy, no? A place of fairness and justice, a place where any sexual orientation, creed, colour, gender, or religion can expect equal treatment under the law. Right?!

ADRIAN does an imitation of THE DEFENSE. THE DEFENSE is well intentioned but overwhelmed by the same system ADRIAN now faces.

THE DEFENSE: I am here to represent . . . umm . . .

Searching through files.

. . . Adrian Ellis in defense of the charges of multiple counts of fraud.

THE DEFENSE settles themselves.

After extensively looking over the files and evidence of the accused crimes, it is my recommendation to my client that we accept a plea deal of eight years imprisonment, decriminalization, and a fine of five thousand dollars.

ADRIAN transitions back.

ADRIAN: We had never been in the same room before and now this lawyer is talking about deals. *(genuinely asking audience)* Why is there no care given for people like us, hmm?

ADRIAN transitions back into THE DEFENSE.

THE DEFENSE: I am on your side. Truly. But we have to look at the seriousness of the charges. Two counts of identity theft and three counts of fraud over five thousand, totaling somewhere in the ballpark of thirty thousand dollars.

ADRIAN transitions back and speaks directly to the audience.

ADRIAN: You are dying to know what the hell is going on, I know. Well, to answer that question, we have to go back, all the way back to the beginning.

Black.

A music box version of "Rock-a-bye Baby" plays.

Adrian Joy was born to unknown people who left the hospital without notifying the staff and were never heard from again. The baby was given a name by the government and put into the system. A system that was never designed with care taken. A system that can consume us.

The music stops.

Now that all sounds super bad . . . and it was. But I was saved from that, by a foster mom named Mama Mavis. I know what you are probably picturing, but don't. Forty, fit, welded for a living, had a sharp tongue and gave no shits about the critical opinions of others. She hated being called Mama Mavis for obvious reasons . . .

Smiling.

But I did it anyway. She was determined from the start to make me feel like I was finally home, regardless of how much I resisted. And I resisted.

Pause.

I came to her at fourteen and put Mama Mavis through hell, trying as hard as I could to push her away. She would always tell me that she was way more stubborn than I was and that she would eventually wear me down. She did . . . with a lot of love and a few whoopins.

Smiles.

Pause as ADRIAN *becomes reflective.*

I spent four years with Mama Mavis and had no idea she was sick. It happened fast *(thoughtfully)* which is good, I guess. The night before my eighteenth birthday, Mavis Ellis made things official and signed adoption papers. That's where the Ellis in my name comes from. Mama gifted it to me. She told me she wanted to make sure I knew who I belonged to. She said she didn't have much, but it would be enough to get me a start on a bright future. A few weeks after she was gone.

Pause.

She was gone and buried before anyone realized.

We can see ADRIAN *reliving the fear of those times.*

But before things got too dark, Mama Mavis sent a gift from the grave. See, near the end she was on disability and well . . . after everything was done, her cheques kept coming. It's amazing how quickly someone can learn new skills when there is money involved. I figured out how to keep the government thinking that Mama was alive. I figured out that if I moved to a very small, scuzzy bachelor apartment and I got a part-time job, there would be enough money left for tuition to a school. To get into the best school possible, I looked at the alumni lists of all of the schools in the area and found someone with the last name Ellis. I learned all the information I needed to know for the applications by snooping the person's feeds and I pretended to be that person's kid and to apply as a legacy. I was determined to get the life Mama wanted for me.

Pause.

This is where I tell you I was guilty.

Pause.

I told the defense the same thing I told you. The defense said considering all that . . . we should definitely accept the prosecution's offer.

Pause.

And that was it. Full stop. I was going to go to jail.

ADRIAN *transitions to* STAR. STAR *is a combination of brilliant corporate lawyer, Black Panther, and ferocious parent advocating for their own child. Although* STAR *is ferocious, she is also genuinely pleasant. This pleasantness comes from a place of extreme confidence in her abilities.*

STAR: *(addressing the room)* Afternoon, folks. My name is Star Mantley Esquire. I work for a corporation called Umoja, and to your detriment, my company has taken a great deal of interest in the case of Adrian Joy Ellis.

STAR holds the room to see if things are clear.

Good. Now, in regards to the offer sent by the prosecution this morning, of which I have a copy here.

Shows the copy.

My future client and I will, as politely as possible, be telling the prosecution to go to hell.

Cutting off the possibility of interruption.

Shhh, shhh, shhh, don't get upset, it's not the right moment. If the prosecution would like to take this to court, we will gladly do so, but that would go poorly for you.

Once again holding the room.

Now this young person allegedly defrauded the government, in the pursuit of what? An education. My company thinks that it is deplorable that local politicians are using this case to show they are tough on crime. Stay with me—30% skilled labour in this city is done by our collective, peoples of African descent. A few years ago these workers formed a union with Umoja and there is enough in their strike fund to sustain a six-month engagement.

STAR is enjoying the position of power.

To stop a long, drawn-out trial and workers' strike, we ask for leniency from the court in the form of a one thousand dollar fine and five hundred hours of community service.

Pause.

Silence.

While you are panicking and calling your bosses to shore up our deal, I will meet with Adrian alone to sign papers formally retaining me as representation. Oh . . . and now you can get upset.

Transitions back into ADRIAN.

ADRIAN: I threw up. Was I being saved here? Why did they care? I don't have any money. What did they want? What the hell was going on? Why me!?

Pause.

ADRIAN *slowly transitions into* STAR.

STAR: *(gently)* Why you? Because care must be given for our collective. Because your story is my story. You're my brother, my auntie, you're me, and I'm you. You're our ancestors and our future. You are part of the collective. Umoja was started by a few wealthy like-minded ancestors, to use the same tactics that have traditionally been used to suppress Black people to elevate us. It has grown to be a Fortune 500 company with holdings in energy, agriculture, manufacturing, shipping, you name it. All of those resources can and are used to fulfill the mandate of care for the collective.

ADRIAN *slowly transitions back for the last time.*

ADRIAN: I was released one hour later with a one thousand dollar fine, five hundred hours of community service, and complete freedom. Star shook my hand and told me my bill would come in the mail in the next few weeks. A letter came that explained I had two options for paying Umoja off. I could perform my five hundred hours of community service at one of their homes that cared for our elders. Or I could sign an attached contract and become part of the collective . . . part of Umoja Corp. They would pay me a nice salary to help others legally figure out the same systems I manipulated. Human capital is the greatest asset of the Umoja Corp.

Pause.

(in sincerity to the audience) So why tell you my story? Why you? Why despite all your troubles and your past, am I talking to you? Why am I talking to you? Because your story is my story. You're my brother, my auntie, you're me, I'm you. You're our ancestors and our future. Care for you will be taken. You are now part of the collective and the skills you possess are now part of us.

ADRIAN *gives a look directly to the audience.*

Welcome to Umoja Corp.

The Umoja chime once again plays and the Umoja symbol is displayed on the screen.

End.

NOTICE

LUKE REECE

Performer: Lisa Berry
Director: Ngozi Paul

I dedicate this piece to those not afraid to change the game and put the world on notice. We need you now more than ever. Let's raise each other up, let's not settle, and let's continue to strive for the best.

ACKNOWLEDGEMENTS

I'd like to acknowledge the many mentors and family members who have supported me throughout my life and made it possible for me to achieve my dream future. You know who you are.

ABOUT THE PLAYWRIGHT

Luke Reece strives to share authentic and engaging stories with audiences through his work as an award-winning playwright, poet, producer, and educator. An advocate for nuanced storytelling that challenges Canadian audiences, Luke is one of Toronto's most decorated slam poets: Toronto Poetry Slam (TPS) Grand Champion in 2017 and winner—twice—of the Canadian Festival of Spoken Word (once as TPS captain, and later, coach). A leader in the national arts community, he represented Canada at the 2019 World Cup of Poetry Slam in Paris, France, where he placed fourth. In 2020, Luke was featured performing for Toronto Raptor and NBA Champion Serge Ibaka on his Instagram Talent Show, *How Talented Are You?* Most recently, Luke's self-directed play, *The Wonderful*, premiered at Caravan Farm Theatre in December 2022, and he is gearing up for several new pieces to take the stage soon.

ARTIST NOTE

Crazy times—but isn't that always the case? Will it always be this crazy?

Our social fabric is on fire, and race politics—including politics around Blackness—and other identity politics are only fuel for this fire.

In *Notice*, we see the future of disenchanted Black children born in this age, their anger and frustration transformed into a powerful agency. They're swift on the court, but are they making the right moves in life? Creating new organizations on the basis of race might not seem like the best way to proceed; on the other hand, it might be the only way.

Sport has long been seen as a way out—but a way out from what?

Black communities have been underserved and overpoliced. Still, we have improved greatly and must continue to improve greatly. Let us think carefully as to how we do that.

I am fascinated by freedom, and taken aback by the divisiveness of this moment, aghast at growing calls for actions that erode what precious freedoms we have enshrined, aghast at certainty in unfounded theories and vigorous destruction in the name of those theories.

Martin Luther King Jr. imagined a world where children of all colours could play, love, and live together. While the dream is still alive, it is not invincible.

What if we used this moment to become our best selves, together?

Perhaps we can imagine a future of equity. *Notice* explores what that future might look like, and how we might win at this game called life, together.

—Ngozi Paul, Director

CHARACTER

Crystal

Interior. Boardroom—day.

CRYSTAL *(thirty-seven) is standing at the front. She speaks to the people.*

CRYSTAL: Have you ever cleaned up a Reese's Peanut Butter Cup after it's been smeared across a laptop screen? I have. It's a moment I'll never forget.

I was twelve years old, a baller held captive indoors by a global pandemic. All I wanted to do was hoop. But even with restrictions lifted over the summer months, *I* wasn't allowed to go to the courts. My dad and I both have asthma, so we were in the "high-risk" category. Practicing my free throws wasn't worth it. I didn't have my own net, so I could only work on handling. I had crossovers like Kyrie, except less *flat-Earth* footed.

My parents tried to support my dream, they just didn't know how. That summer my mom signs me up for an online prep class for student athletes who want to go pro. It's on Zoom, though. Remember Zoom? There's only seven of us in the class, and naturally I'm the only girl, and the only Black kid. The group is mostly hockey and football jocks, including two aspiring NHL players I particularly despise. During the first class one of them asks me out of nowhere if my hair is real, and it rubs me the wrong way. But when the NBA and WNBA seasons restart in the "bubble" and "wobble," respectively, everyone's talking basketball. Because I'm the expert in the room the boys show me *some* respect.

My parents were never into sports, so they see me as an anomaly. My dad is six-foot-eight but nobody could convince him to play sports growing up. All he wanted to do was make candles. I know, right? He's the only candle shop owner who could dunk if he wanted to. The most genuine interest he showed in basketball was when I told him that Drake gave scented candles to the Raptors. While he was making candles, my mother at six-foot-two was putting in serious hours for the Peel Police Special Investigations Unit. So . . . yeah, things were particularly tense around the house that summer.

One day I watch six games back-to-back while my dad exhausts himself trying to figure out the best way to ship his candles internationally. By the time my mom comes home we're passed out on the couch and the house is a mess; no chores done, no dinner ready. The sound of her bag hitting the floor wakes us up. She doesn't say anything to me, only pulls my dad into another room. While overhearing a muffled argument, I notice a Reese's Peanut Butter Cup hanging out of her bag. My mom brings them home for me from a vending machine in her office. To make it up to her, I start to take the prep class seriously.

Then, on August 26, 2020, the NBA hits me different, the first day of the NBA walk-offs. Seeing the game cancellations roll in, it's exhilarating. I'm watching a protest in a way I've never seen before. I've never been so happy *not* to watch basketball.

My class is the next day, and I can't wait until the break so we can discuss the importance of this moment in sports history. However, instead of praising the NBA the two ice boys go off on how "dumb" the league is behaving. They are *enraged* because they wanted to watch the games, and now have nothing to do this afternoon. They even question the intelligence of Hall of Famers like LeBron James and Chris Paul. I'm chewing my Reese's Peanut Butter Cup slowly, waiting for them to give me space to speak.

The break's almost over and one of the boys says: "What difference does it make? The owners have the final say, they always do." And I lose it. I spit out my over-chewed peanut-chocolate chunks at the screen and say "People are dying you fuck-head!" before slamming the laptop shut. My dad is standing at the entrance to my room, shocked. I run past him, grab my basketball, and head out the door without shoes or a mask on. I'm running to the nearest basketball court, I can see it in my sights, can hear Migos beats in the distance, the sound of balls clanking off of backboards ... and then I'm scooped up by my dad's arms. He holds me, and I'm crying. I'm crying like I did when Kobe and Gianna died.

A few days later the games resume, after the league and team owners pledge three hundred million dollars to social justice initiatives. Even back then, it didn't feel like enough. The players seem defeated, despite this apparent victory for the cause. At the time, the NBA was 81.1% Black—but the majority white ownership had all the power. What if that boy was right? The people I looked up to were at the mercy of their masters.

It's decided that I don't return to the class, but my mom doesn't speak to me about what happened. My dad sits me down and talks to me about candles. He tells me that the first burn of a candle is the most important. The entire top layer of wax needs to liquify—if not, then it won't burn evenly. He says that a fire's been lit in me, and we need to let in burn. I tell him, with all my pre-teen angst, that the league has been put on notice.

Fast-forward five years and I'm tearing up the hardwood in high school. My dad has become a student of the game, and my mom comes to see me play when she can. For Christmas that year my dad gets me one of the candles Drake had sent to the Raptors. He used his connections to hunt down the exact brand and make. He even writes on it, with the same sharpie Drake used, the word "Notice." For New Year's Eve, we make our resolutions. Mine is to be seen by a scout, my dad's is to have me be seen by a scout, and my mom's is to be there *when* I'm scouted.

I receive a full ride to South Carolina studying Business & Management. The night before I leave for school my mom takes me out for dinner, and we talk about the incident for the first time. She tells me that summer she worked herself into the ground and was forced into a leave of absence. She would drive around all day instead, and pick up some Reese's Cups so I thought she was still working. All she wanted to do was set a good example for me. She became a police officer to make an impact.

I graduate summa cum laude and lead the NCAA in assists on the way to a title. My parents are with me when I'm drafted in the first round, win defensive player of the year, and eventually the WNBA title. But as much as I love playing the game, I have another trajectory in mind, and they know it, too. Every step of the way my dad reminds me that my candle is still burning, and my mom and I take turns setting examples for each other.

And that continues today, as I stand here twenty-five years after I learned how chocolate can damage a track pad, as the NBA Deputy Commissioner. I've been imagining a new future for Black athletes, and it starts with basketball.

Today is June 19, 2045—180 years since the abolishment of slavery in the United States. I called this meeting today because we have the power to make choices that shift the face of sports across the globe. There is more wealth in Black hands than ever before, but until we release these teams from old white hands, athletes will not be free to use their influence fully. What good is a wick if you can't light it?

You know, there's a common mistake that's made when putting out the flame of a candle—blowing it out. It seems like the easy solution, but it's actually best if you snuff it. When you blow, it sends hot wax everywhere, creating new fires you didn't even know about. Those are the dangerous ones. That's how *my* candle was lit.

I'm here to tell you that the Black NBA and WNBA players, joined by a contingent of non-Black players and allies, will work for *this* league no more. We're leaving. We have formed a new basketball league, a new *standard*, under Black ownership and Black management. Players, coaches, and executives are all resigning right now. The best athletic talents of our generation have already agreed to play for us, *the* basketball association.

This is a league where we can *speak up* and dribble, a league that fully embraces our humanity, and our freedom.

There is no discussion. This is not a warning, not even an ultimatum. You have no more power over us—Notice? We gave you that twenty-five years ago.

End.

BLACKBERRIES

MIALI-ELISE COLEY-SUDLOVENICK

Performer: Adeline Bird
Director: Alicia K. Harris

When I think of my personal story, I feel an appreciation for my grandparents' journeys. I dedicate *Blackberries* my late maternal grandparents, Davidee Uluakallak and Mary (Murray) Davidee, and my late paternal grandparents, Lester Coley Sr. and Doreen Elease (Weathers Coley) Dwyer. Their stories allowed me to continue mine.

ABOUT THE PLAYWRIGHT

Miali-Elise Coley-Sudlovenick was born and raised in Iqaluit, Nunavut. Miali loves to spend time with her family on the land berry-picking, clam-digging, or being at their cabin. Finding ways to celebrate her Inuk Jamaican intersectionality encourages Miali to create a legacy for her children to feel safe and connected in their communities. As an educator and fluent Inuktitut teacher, Miali teaches through her business, Allurvik. In 2018 Miali created the first Inuktitut podcast, *Tusaavisii?*. Away from teaching and spending time on the land, Miali has a passion for food and the arts, especially those inspired by her Inuit and Jamaican heritages. In February 2023, Miali received the African Descent Person of Excellence in Nunavut Award from the Nunavut Black History Society.

ARTIST NOTE

Many of us have intersecting identities. In *Blackberries*, we see Effie reflect on her mixed-heritage family, her two cultures. The play follows her journey in uniting the two, as she embraces them both as herself, both as home. Effie shows us it's never too late to learn more about your heritage, to grow and to expand—as there is no one way to be Black. Black future is us reclaiming our roots, freely. Black future is us being accepted as we are, and all parts of ourselves. Black future is redefining home.

—Alicia K. Harris, Director

CHARACTER

Effie

Exterior. Land—day.

EFFIE is getting out of a small boat. Fixing her dishevelled, windblown hair. She is with her cousin Tia, and they are down the bay, on the remote sections of land outside the town/city. They have only just crossed the bay and have docked on a hillside terrain.

EFFIE: Now *this* is nature! Makes sense why you'd come here to berry-pick! Away from town and everything. So fresh!

EFFIE looks around.

I wish we came sooner. No one can bug us out here! Except these damn mosquitos!

She swats away a mosquito, pauses, looks around, and takes in the moment. She smells the air, chuckles lightly. Looking down at the berries, she kneels down, and puts her bucket next to a patch of berries.

Tia! There's soooo many berrrriesss! Where do I even start!?

She takes a closer look. Pause.

Waaait! You call these blackberries? These are crowberries, or that's what we call them in BC! Uncle said we'd be picking blackberries.

Surprised, she keeps the first few berries in her hand, looks up at her cousin picking, and puts some berries in her mouth.

(after tasting a few) They seem smaller, but these are definitely crowberries.

You know what, who cares, blackberries, crowberries, these are delicious!

Pause.

I bet our grandparents felt this connection to the land. Complete sense of freedom, no strict schedule. Living day by day. Plus, no alcohol . . . seems so hard to imagine now, but so normal once upon a time. Man, it was so hard getting up this morning. That vodka was a bad idea.

She makes a puke expression.

Yuck.

Pause.

But I don't regret this. Stellar view. Seems a little strange without trees, haha. Kinda naked. Ha!

She sighs in disbelief at how beautiful it is.

I wish Aja came with us. I love her, but *man* can she drink! She cracks me up, just says anything.

Pause.

Have you thought about living further south for a bit? You could stay with me. I think you'd like it. Get a break from all the people at your house. Who even lives there!? I think I'd lose it if people came to visit whenever. Seems weird. But bonus when someone brings drinks, eh. We've been drunk every day since the funeral . . . shia . . . that was what . . . two weeks ago?!

Pause.

I'm getting tired of drinking though. Promise I'll take a break when I'm home. I'm leaving in *two days*?! You know what, to celebrate my first time berry-picking in Nunavut, I'm taking a break . . . Sober, starting today!

Pause. She looks around.

Aja would love it out here.

(hesitant) Who knows, maybe she'd take a break from drinking too?

Pause. No response from Tia.

(feeling embarrassed) You know what . . . I'm sorry. I want Aja, you, all of us to be healthy! If that's being sober, why not? . . . I mean, if you want?! I just want better things for us. Sounds dumb, doesn't it? Sorry, I'm blabbing.

Pause.

Check it out! . . . your bucket's almost full! I need to catch up! I'll pick enough to bring to Aja . . . Uncle says she makes the best jam! Maybe she could teach me!? Is one bucket enough for a few jars?! I bet Aja's jam tastes way better than Mom's.

She smirks.

Pause.

I can't believe Mom won't come back here, not even for her mother's funeral! Who does that!?

She shakes her bucket with frustration.

Aja said Mom was too hurt to ever come back.

But I wish I came up sooner, to meet Grandma. She was really special, wasn't she? The funeral was packed! I bet everyone knew her.

Pause.

Tia, thanks for listening. I guess you're not really used to this, eh . . . cousin flies in, hangs out every day, then lets it all out when you take her berry-picking? Haha. Blackberries, freaking blackberries, got me talking away!

Pause.

Hmmmm, I've never told anyone this . . . but a few years ago at my parents' place, I heard Mom upstairs. She was talking to someone in Inuktitut. She'd pause to listen, then yell a word that sounded like "summa." She kept repeating it. Whoever it was, was making her mad. She started crying. She put the phone on speaker, sounded like an old man. You know . . . I never heard her cry like that . . . ever.

Pauses.

(frustrated) I couldn't take it anymore, so I ran upstairs, you know, to give her a hug. She looked at me . . . like she was embarrassed. Then she told me to get out.

She shakes her lowered head. Pause.

When I got to town, Uncle met me up at the airport. He gave me the biggest hug I'd ever had. He said I looked like my mom.

(tad annoyed) When he was driving me to Aja's place I asked if he knew what "summa" means. "Why?" he asked, as if he was asking me why I wanted to know. *(chuckling)* Then I realized "summa" actually meant "why."

She chuckles lightly.

Pause.

Hmmmm . . . Mom always made me think there was nothing up here. Except for all the drinking. Probably 'cause that's all she saw from Grandpa. Aja said he passed away a few years ago, but Mom didn't tell us. I thought I'd meet him. Tia, it makes sense . . . that phone call, it was Grandpa!

Pause.

You know . . . after all this, I can say I've berry-picked! Sure, I'll need to learn much more, because honestly Mom didn't tell us about her life up here. And . . . to think of it . . . we didn't learn about us in school. *Hmmmm* . . . maybe a couple days, here and there, but that was it! I used to think it was only us Black people who felt unseen . . . unheard . . . but even people who lived here first . . . ugh!

She's frustrated.

Pause.

You have no idea how much I needed this. Been interrupted my whole life. My thoughts are so clear.

She takes a breath.

Knowing you really hear me . . . you see me . . . and that I matter.

Pause.

I could do this everyday, e-v-e-r-y-day . . . it's the best I've ever felt.

As EFFIE *continues to berry-pick, she hears a soft, meditative sound in the distance. It's so quiet that for a moment all she hears is the rhythm of her heart beating. It continues to grow into a gutteral throatsinging that overlaps and continues into African sounds of throatsinging.* EFFIE *takes in the moment by looking around and feels the connections in the sounds.*

Wow, I feel the sounds of the land. Being Black in Canada and having Inuit roots, I belong somewhere, for the first time, I'm here!

Pause.

Is it too late?

Pause.

(confidently) I'm going to learn Inuktitut. Teach me everything you know! I know the word for berry-picking, because I heard you say it: Nu-ni-vak *[nnoo-knee-vuk]*. Hehe.

Pause.

Hearing you speak Inuktitut—wow—I just had to be here.

EFFIE *recalls more of her Black roots by seeing Inuit thriving in their language and culture.* EFFIE *knows the connections are strong and wants to embrace the fullness of her identities. Being Black and Inuk, the languages hold the cultural understandings of her identities.*

Pause.

I can't go back to BC, but I have to. Then I'll come back.

Tia, if Mom didn't call me about Grandma, I wouldn't be here.

She stands up and looks around.

But I think I understand why Mom didn't come back, and that's okay!

Pause.

Mmmmm, guess what!? I'll bring some jam back for Mom, she'll be so impressed I made jam! Ha! She always says I'm a terrible cook, says I'd die if I had to fend for myself. Whatever! Jam's a staple.

Pause.

Tia . . . I could live here. Sure, the drinking and crowded living can't be easy, but look at us now! We are berry-picking, Nu-ni-vak-tuguk *[Nnoo-knee-vuk- two-gok]*. Haha!

She looks around for the final time.

I needed this . . . I've never been happier . . . I love this place!

She chuckles and smiles at her cousin and walks off stage.

EMMETT

SYRUS MARCUS WARE

Performer: Prince Amponsah
Director: Tanisha Taitt

I wrote this play for my daughter, Amelie, and for my father, Edgar Ware, and my grandfather, Harold Irons, for my community, and for all of us—as we made our way through a pandemic and a slew of racial uprisings and the beginning of the revolutionary moment we now find ourselves in. This play is also dedicated to Emmett Till and Medgar Evers, whose memory I hope to keep alive as we continue Medgar's struggle for freedom, with Emmett Till's love and joy.

ACKNOWLEDGEMENTS

This play was brought to life with the help of director Tanisha Taitt and actor Prince Amponsah—together we co-created an experience of a near future where Black disabled people have survived. "Against all odds and in the most unlikely of ways," as Medgar says in the play, we survive. I am thankful to Tanisha and Prince for their care with this work and their magic. I am thankful to Luke Reece for first connecting with me about this project and to Mumbi and the entire Obsidian Theatre Company team for making this dream a reality and for supporting my work. Thank you to the CBC for supporting our work and creating access for so many to see Black stories and Black futures every day.

ABOUT THE PLAYWRIGHT

Syrus Marcus Ware is a Vanier Scholar, visual artist, activist, curator, and educator. Syrus is Assistant Professor at the School of the Arts, McMaster University. Using painting, installation, and performance, Syrus works with and explores social justice frameworks and Black activist culture and has shown widely in galleries and festivals across Canada. He is part of the Performance Disability Art Collective and is a co-founder of Black Lives Matter—Canada and the Wildseed Centre for Art & Activism. Syrus is a past co-curator of Blackness Yes!/Blockorama and current lead of the Wildseed Black Arts Fellowship. He is co-editor (with Rodney Diverlus and Sandy Hudson) of *Until We Are Free: Reflections on Black Lives Matter in Canada* (University of Regina Press, 2020).

ARTIST NOTE

How fascinating it is for Obsidian to consider the future of Blackness through so many pairs of our own eyes. It has been an incredible experience collaborating with Syrus Marcus Ware and Prince Amponsah on *Emmett*. From the first time I read the piece, I was struck by its beautiful and stark imagery. What is Blackness when humanity is all but a memory? What energy does Black love—and Black love lost—leave behind? In *Emmett*, a Black man who should be dead is somehow still alive. That simple statement is the story of the Black spirit itself: it—we—are not gone. In the face of all that would seek to erase it—and the bodies inhabited by it—it remains unbreakable, indomitable, wounded but glorious, and defiantly Black.

—Tanisha Taitt, Director

CHARACTERS

Medgar

Exterior. Undetermined place—day.

MEDGAR *wanders through the forest collecting bark, sticks, and twigs. He is wearing a makeshift fishing line that rests against his back. A bag rests on his hip, the strap running across his chest up to his shoulder. We hear his voice.*

MEDGAR: *(voice-over)* It's been seven years exactly since the Fall. I normally spend today remembering the past, honouring our dead and marvelling that I, somehow, survived.

I do it alone, you know? It feels private somehow. I mean, I guess we do everything alone, now.

I like to light candles. I normally do the same thing on this day, as I remember. But this year everything is different.

(excitedly) Today is not about the past!

It's about the future. Today they found life on Venus!

Not the traces of life's "residue" like they found in 2020. Remember that? How excited we were? No—this is actual life—living beings that we are going to be able to communicate with. They are sending more transmissions tonight. I can hardly believe it. My transmitter is charging now so that I can tune in tonight.

We are not alone.

Live talking begins.

Not alone. Not alone!

The Fall claimed so many of us. The majority of the Earth's population fell and we who are left are scattered around the globe, living off whatever we can find. In what was T'karon:to, the former cityscape exists as a large peninsula that stands in the massive Great Ontario Sea.

The Humber River and Don flooded T'karon:to and met with Lake Ontario and northern waterways to form the sea, which stretches as far east as what was once the St. Lawrence River. Our peninsula is long, maybe a hundred kilometres. And it is wide and covered in forest.

In the edges of the dense forests lining the shores, I make my way.

> MEDGAR *arrives at the site of his annual ritual (centre stage) and crouches down. He begins making a fire while talking. He breaks kindling and stacks it into a triangle peak, stuffing leaves under the wood to ignite.*

I was never naive enough to think that it would be me who survived an apocalypse. In all the stories you read, the protagonist always has *just* what it takes—timing and skill to be able to avoid the worst. We assumed we too would survive any eventuality.

I saw the flaw in that—the false hope—the futility of imagining that of all the billions of humans on Earth I would be the one spared. And so I lived my life knowing that when shit really got bad, I likely wouldn't survive. I would try, sure, but the odds were stacked against me.

Emmett, you were so sure you could survive anything. It's one of the first things I loved about you.

> MEDGAR *pauses.*

The universe has a way of showing us up at every turn.

> MEDGAR *gets fire to light.*

I survived.

> *The fire crackles.* MEDGAR *sits.*

Against all odds and in the most unlikely of ways, I survived the Fall. Me. My disabled, chronically ill, and immunocompromised self survived the Fall. The virus to end all viruses. And I am alone. More alone than I've ever been before.

MEDGAR pauses.

It's weird living in a forest with no birds. An avian virus wiped out all birds maybe four years ago. It's made the Earth eerily silent. I never really noticed how much a part of our white noise, background noise, they were. Maybe even more than cars and traffic.

There is a bird call. The gentle wail of a loon.

I remember lying in bed in the mornings at my grandparents' house . . . they lived off this lake. There was a loon nesting ground and they would fly over the house every morning around 7:30. That particular cry only loons make.

It's hard to imagine: all birds, gone.

They just fell from the sky. At one point the ground was littered with dead birds across the forest floor by this lake. And then bones everywhere—carcasses decaying. And then nothing.

And there was silence.

The sound of the loon trails off.

So much silence.

MEDGAR remembers.

I have three feathers! I found them in the underbrush on a walk shortly after the birds fell. To hold them . . . they are so soft, you know? They allow for flight . . .

It's hard to imagine that they will never again exist.

(matter-of-factly) The world is quiet.

MEDGAR stands.

But now, as of today, we will no longer be alone.

We may not even have to stay on the Earth. As of today, the scientists watching the stars confirm that they have made contact with the folks on Venus.

(excitedly) Imagine, leaving Earth? I never was one of those people. The Mars enthusiasts, the ones who wanted to just bail and find another planet to contaminate. I wasn't an environmentalist, per say, but I'd always been firm that I'd rather stay and try to heal this place. I know you loved the idea of Mars . . . and I wanted to stay here.

This Earth. Our home.

In the end, it's done a great job of healing itself.

(slight laughter) With the majority of the world's population gone, the water runs clean, industry has stopped, and the air is returning to normal. Everything is green and expansive.

Life is returning to a balance on this planet. It's the perfect time to stay here—if not for the viruses.

I remember when the worst one hit, the one that ultimately caused the Fall. Terrifyingly lethal.

It still lingers. It still kills. It still has a slow spread. And we know there will just be more coming.

> *MEDGAR walks away from the fire, towards the shore looking out at the water. He is still. Considering. He washes his hands in the water. He picks up sand in his hand and lets it fall from his fingers.*

But life out in space? That is impossible to imagine!

I mean . . . those that went to Mars died within the first year.

They will be broadcasting the communication with Venus tonight.

EMMETT

Today. On the anniversary of the Fall. On the anniversary of losing you . . . today we will meet a possible future—something we have never before dreamed.

He picks up some more sand in his hands.

This shoreline used to be Eglinton. The street that never stopped being contested. The street that was my home. The street where all the Black people lived. Little Jamaica.

Home. I sought out where the street met this shoreline, chose to make home *here.* Like somehow being where I grew up would be safer—though nothing about this place is as it was then.

Remember my love, when we lived there together?

So much has changed since the Fall. I wish you were here with me. I wanted to make this recording—

Voice cracks. He steadies himself. The water laps up against the shoreline and hits the rocks.

I wanted to make this recording in case— What—

He tries to steady himself again, but falls to his knees.

That somehow in some parallel dimension you can hear this and know that I remembered you? That I never forgot? Hell, if there's life on Venus, maybe there's a way that you're out there still—as energy, in our atmosphere—in the stardust?

Why couldn't we have both broken the odds? What is the point of a future here, in space, anywhere without you?

Emmett. I love you. End recording.

MEDGAR *stands and touches the recording device, saving the recording.*

End.

GEORGEENA

DJANET SEARS

Performer: Virgilia Griffith
Director: Weyni Mengesha

ABOUT THE PLAYWRIGHT

Djanet Sears is a playwright, director, and a part-time lecturer at the University of Toronto. Her work has graced such stages as the National Arts Centre, Mirvish Productions, Tarragon Theatre, Nightwood Theatre, Obsidian Theatre Company, Black Theatre Workshop, Centaur Theatre, Soulpepper Theatre, the Public Theatre, Stratford Shakespeare Festival, Crossroads Theatre, the Royal Shakespeare Company, The Grand Theatre, St. Louis Black Repertory, Canadian Stage, and Factory Theatre. Sears has been awarded several honours including a Governor General's Literary Award, Canadian Screenwriting Award, Chalmers Canadian Play Award, Dora Mavor Moore Award, Martin Luther King Jr. Achievement Award, and a Gold Prize at the International Radio Festival of New York. She is a founding member of the Obsidian Theatre Company, and the editor of two anthologies: *Testifyin': Contemporary African Canadian Drama, Vols. I & II*. Her best known plays, *Harlem Duet* and *The Adventures of a Black Girl in Search of God*, have been widely published and translated.

ARTIST NOTE

In the wake of the murders of George Floyd and Breonna Taylor, when race-based incidents are investigated in the media, it is common practice for journalists to examine the motivations of the perpetrators. We see it happening in the news today in reports about the Capitol insurrection. We saw it when a Canadian "Karen," Amy Cooper, called the police on a birdwatcher in Central Park: "Why did (insert name of a Karen here) feel forced to attack (a description of a person of colour here)?" But do we know the name of the man she victimized? His last name was Cooper too—Christian Cooper. Another frequently asked question is: "What is behind the rise in race-based attacks on people of colour?" Or: "What drove (insert the name of a "Kevin"—a wannabe fascist—here) to want to be a Proud Boy?" If the injured party is Black, the news story will typically focus on the white attacker.

This short play was inspired by real events. It was also prompted by a two-decade-old study out of Duke University Medical Center by clinical psychologist Maya McNeilly, which suggested that "racist provocation" could lead to damaging physical and emotional symptoms. As McNeilly put it, "It is well-documented that racism has negative social, economic and political consequences on African Americans, but the direct effects of racism on physical and emotional health have only begun to be explored."

This story continues that exploration and contemplates the effects of the terrorism that overt and implicit white supremacy has on the physical and emotional life of one particular Black woman: Georgeena.

—Djanet Sears, Playwright

CHARACTERS

Geena Darsan

Canada Day. Late Night. Highway 400, Ontario.

GEENA *Darsan, thirty-seven, grips the steering wheel hard. She is silent. The drone of the car engine envelops* GEENA *and drowns out the faint bursts of fireworks on the horizon that intermittently perforate the night sky, lighting up the darkness.*

The phone rings.

She refuses to look in the direction of the singing phone and makes every effort to keep her gaze on the roadway ahead. She hardly blinks. She stares ahead of her, almost imperceptibly shaking her head, as if her brain is replaying a scene she does not wish to revisit. The faint sound of GEENA*'s heart beating begins to form a rhythm section to the constant drone of vehicular white noise and the ringing phone. The tempo of her heartbeat gets faster.*

A flash of neon arteries and veins radiating from deep inside her appear and disappear.

Beads of sweat form on her face. She glances over at the centre console, reaches to turn up the a/c, and loses control of the vehicle for a millisecond. She quickly makes the correction. The phone stops ringing. The sound of her heartbeat begins to fade.

GEENA *pulls off her recently acquired Vivica Fox bob, and the wig cap underneath, and tosses them onto the back seat. They land on the small pile of sparklers and handheld Canadian flags beside her designer overnight bag.*

GEENA*'s shoulder-length locks fall all around her. She removes several strands covering her face.*

She reaches behind her back, and with some difficulty, unhooks her bra. She slips one arm through the bra straps one at a time under her top. She flings the bra onto the back seat. With one hand still on the wheel, she wrestles to peel herself out of her girdle. She manages to get the tight-fitting foundation garment down to the top of her hips, then gives up the losing battle.

She removes a high-heeled sandal from her left foot. She places the now-bare foot on the accelerator and removes the other shoe from her driving foot. She throws the shoes onto the passenger-side floor.

The sound of her phone ringing again pierces the white noise.

GEENA*'s jaw tightens. Her heart beats faster again. The faint network of neon arteries and veins become apparent, but for longer this time. They pulse to the polyrhythmic beat created by her heartbeat and the ringing phone.*

She takes a deep breath, glances over at her trembling purse on the passenger seat beside her. Then, making every effort to keep her eyes on the road, GEENA *carefully reaches for her purse. It's beyond her grasp. She trains her eyes on the yellow line in front of her, unlocks her seat belt, extends her arm, and leans towards the adjacent seat. She locates the purse and slips her hand inside.*

A light emanates from the soft leather tote, illuminating the darkness. She retrieves the phone and the ringing stops abruptly.

She sets the phone on her lap. She dials, only glancing down from time to time to ensure she's pressed the correct button. The dialled number begins to ring.

MATHIEW: *(off stage)* This is Mathiew Spruyce. Obviously I can't get to the phone right now. So please leave a message, or send me an email to mathiewspruyce@mailbox.ca. That's M.A.T.H.I.E.W.S.P.R.U.Y.C.E. at mailbox dot—

She presses End. The car has begun to veer out of its lane. She quickly adjusts the steering.

GEENA leans in the direction of the passenger seat, rummages inside her purse, takes out a single-sided earphone, and places it in her ear.

She pulls her seat belt over her chest but has trouble locking it with one hand.

The phone rings. She abandons the seat belt and presses the Bluetooth option on the phone in her lap.

GEENA: No, no, no. No—No, no . . . I am not a cockroach! Cockroaches do not drink wine from long stem glasses. Cockroaches cannot tell the difference between a zinfandel and a shiraz. Cockroaches don't earn PhDs and run their own labs at the university. Even if she believed— We were eating. We were having dinner and she— No, don't you dare, don't you dare—I don't care that she used to be a zoologist. That research is so goddamn old. First, cockroaches did not come to the new world with Africans on slave ships. Second—sec—that, that, that scholarship is blatantly wrong. Fossilized cockroaches have been carbon-dated in Europe, Asia, Australia, and the Americas. They are forty-four to forty-nine million years old. So the notion that cockroaches accompanied my, my tortured and abducted ancestors like some, some kind of invited guest.

The network of arteries and veins slowly reappear, and can be seen through her clothes and skin and flesh. A blister appears on the surface of her chest, near her neck.

And I even checked. Afterwards I checked. 'Cause this kind of accusation . . . this kind of shit always makes you think it's you. For a second I thought I must have made it up—No, I was the cockroach in your mother's analogy. All Black people were the cockroach.

GEENA touches the blister with her finger. The area is tender.

I do not care that she adopted you when you were a baby. I don't care that she loves you. I don't care that I was the first Black woman you'd ever brought home! I don't care about the goddamn dress. I don't care that 153 friends and family members will descend on your family's home tomorrow. I don't. I was—I was sitting at your family's magnificent ivory-and-blackwood dining table, the day before my wedding, defending whether the lives of Black people goddamn matter, for god's—

The network of arteries disappears, leaving only the wound on her chest.

Of course all lives matter. You know that. Why can't they hear the implied "too" when it comes to Black lives? Black lives matter . . . too! Black lives matter too— And that's a problem. That's a very big problem. You said absolutely nothing. How the hell can you understand where she's coming from— He had skittles and iced tea in his pocket, for Christ's sake, Mathiew. We went to the march during the lockdown. I thought . . . you could've, you should've, you didn't have my back— Telling, telling your mother that there are two sides to every . . . That is not having my back! There are not two sides. Okay, no, no . . . there *are* two sides. The right side and the goddamn wrong one. Your mother is so— We're talking about, we were discussing the execution of a twelve-year-old human child. Jesus Chri— She was accusing me of not being open to discussing . . . how is . . . how is cutting off oxygen to a human being the appropriate punishment for selling cigarettes without a license? Why is this even a discussion— She's hurt? What? I did not call her a racist. 'Cause god forbid you call a racist a racist. Negotiating the right *of Black people to live is okay.* But calling— When your father said he doesn't see colour, did I say anything. Did I? No. I was a good ole Negro. So what exactly does he see when he looks at me? You are your father's Black son. Adopted Black son. Does he see you as white? I want you to know that it took everything, everything in me not to slap your brother. "Take Canada Back"? You have a white brother who's going to vote for a Reform conservative putz that wants to "Take Canada Back"? Take it back from who? And his gallerina wife posing with that Make America Great Again hat. That hat is not a joke. And that's supposed to be funny? He thinks it's funny? And I'm dying inside. And you laugh.

GEENA tries pulls her seat belt on again.

You're laughing with him like a good little Negro.

Her skirt appears to be covering the seat belt buckle holder.

Then I defend myself and suddenly your mother's all hurt, and suddenly it's all about her tears.

She lets the seat belt buckle go.

She calls me a cockroach and it's my fault she's crying. I did not call her a racist. 'Cause we all know that calling any of them racist would be worse than Sandra losing her life, or Breonna being murdered just 'cause the police barged into the wrong house. Ha. White tears, Black lives—

Her reaction to what he's saying makes her lose control of the vehicle. She makes a quick recovery.

Don't you dare, no. I've always . . . I've always been that, that proud Negro, that cultured Negro who uses her intellect to convince people like that to, to see . . . see me . . . Everything I do. Everything I've done is about convincing them . . . I'm human. I'm human too. But when she . . . at best she was blaming Black people for cockroaches. At worst she was admitting that's how she saw us. And I don't care that she's worked on herself, worked on her biases. She thinks of me as a cockroach. Your intelligent cockroach girlfriend. Your charming cockroach wife-to-be. And it just came out—

The network of arteries inside her body are visible again.

Yes—yes, I did. I told your mother, "Fuck you." I told your father, "Fuck you." I told your brother and his wife, "Fuck you." The wine glass was in my hand. I'll pay to get the stains removed. Because I should've known better. It's better to sit there sipping shiraz, negotiating with you, with your mother, about whether white people have the right to take my life—that it's better for me just to sit quietly and try to understand why they think white people have a right to kill me. And it happens every day. Usually they're more subtle. More *insidious* . . . like paper cuts. Most Black people average thirteen race-based paper cuts a day.

Welts emerge from the intersection of blood vessels and skin.

Sometimes more. That's over 4,700 race cuts a year. Nearly fifty thousand cuts a decade. Most scab over quickly and heal. Some ooze at first. The psyche tries to push out the toxins, and the skin has to bind the exit wounds. And paper cuts hurt in a way that other cuts don't. It's the nerve endings. There are so many nerve endings on the skin, on the hands, fingers. It's more painful. They hurt even after they heal. Some never heal at all. And then there's the terror of it. The terror of wounds yet to come. Will the salesperson . . . Will the doctor . . . I live with that terror every fucking day.

Even more welts begin to appear.

My psyche is a galaxy of scars. My soul is a burn victim. And when you get scarred, your skin gets tight, thin, brittle, inflexible. Touch me the wrong way at times, too harshly, without consideration, and I will crack and my insides will seep out. I will not live like that—

The welts erupt.

Don't you dare . . . I tried. I always try. I've worn my best Vivica Fox wig to every family event. I have a PhD, yet every time I see your family, I have to spend so much time on my goddamn makeup—

GEENA *is now covered in barely visible scars.*

I'm not blaming you, Mathiew. I'm blaming me. What am I doing watching makeup tutorials? I've replayed one video so many times I can recite it by heart. I am contoured to the FUCKING gods. My cheekbones . . . The bridge of my nose looks so sculpted, so thin, you'd think I was Meryl Streep playing Nina Simone. And of course a pinky-blush lipstick, not the deep browns I love. You hate the browns. I know you hate the browns—you kiss me more when I'm not wearing browns, and I'm not blaming you. But . . . I don't know. I don't know. I'm tired. I'm tired of smiling in the face of this shit. It's not what I want for my life. Not my personal, my intimate life. I don't want to hide my hair when I leave my house. I don't want to disguise the bridge of my nose. I no longer want to hide the umber, brown, ebony, black of me just for people to treat me— To see me as more like them. More human. To see me not as a cockroach . . .

GEENA *sees the eruptions. She sees the scars. She gently rubs the affected areas.*

I'll call them first thing—yep. I'll send out a, a mass email or something when I get— Just call the pastor. If guests show up—

Her eyes become a river.

Yes— Yep— Can you call the pastor?

A stream delicately carves its way down her cheek and onto her lips.

Okay—'kay—uh-huh.

Her weeping becomes sobs. This is not a pretty cry. It is full of brackish water, snot and spit. She struggles to hold the steering wheel.

She takes several deep breaths.

Do not confuse my tears with regret. I was crying . . . I am crying because . . . I love you, you know. I'm just crying because—

Flashing lights and a siren interrupt her.

Shit! Gotta go.

GEENA *touches the phone.*

MATHIEW: *(off stage)* What? Geena?! Geena!!

GEENA *ends the call and allows the phone to slip from her lap onto the floor.*

She steers the car to the shoulder of the highway. The flashing lights and sirens follow her.

She begins to reach into the back seat for her wig, but thinks better of it.

She puts both hands on the steering wheel in such a way that it's clear she has nothing in them. She notices the seat belt dangling beside her.

GEENA: Oh shit!

She nervously takes the seat belt and buckles it. Her heart begins to beat loudly. Her arteries become vivid and clear. The network of blood vessels shudders and shakes.

She goes to grab the steering wheel again, but thinks better of it and places her hands in the air.

The sound of her heart beating is deafening. A bright, flashing light shines on her through the driver's side window.

Whiteout.

REBIRTH OF THE AFRONAUTS

MOTION

Performer: Chelsea Russell
Director: Jerome Kruin

To Mom
and Dad

ACKNOWLEDGEMENTS

Many thanks to Mumbi Tindyebwa and Obsidian Theatre for this epic journey. To my collaborators for bringing these words and worlds to life—director Jerome Kruin for the visionary execution, multi-gifted Chelsea Russell for channelling the voices with kinetic energy, and composer NON for the original score, a sonic voyage through the cosmic frequencies of both inner and outer space. And to the visionaries, sound travellers, and funk terrestrials, from the Ancients to the Afrofuture . . .

ABOUT THE PLAYWRIGHT

Motion is an award-winning playwright, screenwriter, poet, and emcee, fusing word, sound, and drama for the stage and screen. She is co-writer of the Canadian Screen Award–winning feature film *Akilla's Escape* with director Charles Officer, which premiered in 2020 at TIFF, and writer of ReelWorld Award–winning short film *A Man's Story*, which has screened in film festivals across the globe. Her most recent production for the stage is *Oraltorio: A Theatrical Mixtape* with DJ L'Oqenz, which premiered at the RISER Project, remounted with Obsidian Theatre Company/ Soulpepper, and played at both CINARS in Montreal and the Chale Wote Festival in Ghana. Motion's other notable works include *Aneemah's Spot* (SummerWorks/ BAND TD Festival) and the Dora Mavor Moore Award–nominated *Nightmare Dream* (IFT Theatre/Obsidian). She has been published in *Motion in Poetry* and *40 Dayz* (Women's Press), *Everything Remains Raw* (Goose Lane Editions), and *The Black Notes* (Insomniac Press). As a writer and producer for film and TV, she has worked on the television series *Coroner* (CBC/CW), *Diggstown* (CBC), and the CSA Award–winning series *Revenge of the Black Best Friend* (Amanda Parris/iThentic/ CBC Gem). She is also creator and course director of *Griots to Emcees: Culture, Performance & Spoken Word* at York University in Toronto.

ARTIST NOTE

Rebirth of the Afronauts: A Black Space Odyssey incorporates themes that are rarely explored in mainstream media: Afrofuturism, Afrofuturist music, reparations, space travel, destiny, and the future of language and technology with respect to identity and the African diaspora in North America. These themes and storylines in *Rebirth* are essential; they are rooted in history, while amplifying the voice of the next generation.

In mainstream media, I have not seen a film or TV show talking about reparations, reclamation of land, and Black liberation in an Afrofuturist world, and especially not from a Canadian point of view.

The film asks bold questions about who we are as individuals, as people, as a culture, and as a nation. To be a first- or second-generation African Canadian is to experience identity at the intersections of nation and ethnicity. I ask myself those same questions all the time, and as a proud first-generation African Canadian director sought to bring my unique vision and authenticity to the film.

I am extremely honoured to have collaborated with Motion—a super-talented writer, wise beyond my imagination—and the generous Chelsea Russell, a talented ball of energy and force to be reckoned with.

—Jerome Kruin, Director

CHARACTERS

Chariott
'Lo
Swiing

and
the Voice of BlackSpaceX Radio

Samples, Sound Bites, and Sound Effects

Mission Control
Malcolm x
Sun Ra
Col. Nkoloso
CBC Announcer
Subway
Drivah
The B-Wimmin

(voices are indicated by double parentheses—(( ))—and can be samples, sound bites, pre-recorded, played live by a DJ, or interpolated by the actor)

Voice-overs can be utilized at points in the script to convey a filmic narration.

INTRO.

A small room, Tkaronto, Reparations Eve, 2059 A.D.

CHARIOTT stands in a column of dim light. A mastermix of sounds around her.

On screen, numbers scroll, counting upward. "Uploading to the cloud . . . %"

Intercut medley of SFX, sound bites, shortwave samples, moon-landing and space launch sounds:

BLACKSPACEX RADIO: Altitude, velocity, light!

MISSION CONTROL: ((T minus fifteen seconds . . .))

MALCOLM X: ((There are Black people . . . able to toss sputniks out there in the atmosphere, out in space . . .))

COL. NKOLOSO: ((D'kalu . . . Uhruru . . . Entoto . . .))

SUN RA: ((They take frequent trips to the moon . . .))

SWIING: Belt. Boots. Backpack. Wings . . . You're not going nowhere without your wings.

Static pulse from CHARIOTT's inner shortwave. She rouses and moves her body to tune in to a faraway station. AFROFUTURISTIC TUNE comes in.

On screen: EQ lights move.

BLACKSPACEX RADIO: . . . And for y'all having a quiet New Year's Eve—say goodbye to the last night of the '50s. New Year, New We. Crossing you over to Reparations Day. Gonna channel your cosmos, with Georgia Anne Muldrow, some Ras G. Then throw it way back to last century—Earth Wind and Fire, Brides of Funkenstein, "(Star Child) Mothership Connection." So no fear, my frozen ones, your Seer is here. Live from the astralight. With the sounds that keep you lit. *(echo)*

RADIO DROP: ((W.S.P.A.C.Eeeeee. Broadcasting from BlackSpaceX . . . x . . . x . . .))

CHARIOTT's cell goes off. On screen: "No [Caller] ID" (or some unrecognizable symbols). She jumps out of her cloud-state, reads digits on her palm, answers with a flick of her wrist.

CHARIOTT: Yeah?

BLACKSPACEX RADIO: Congratulations! You have won a trip on the Mothership!

STATIC. CLICK. A high-pitched sound, like the skin-curdling whine of a giant mechanical mosquito, grows and fades. Cacophony rises over static shortwave pulse—unbearable.

CHARIOTT ejects out of the portal. It closes behind her with a BANG! She turns back. Can't get back in, so gotta move on . . .

TRACK I.

The streets. Night.

On screen: Tkaronto, Dec. 31, 2059 A.D. / 39 A.G. (Year of Our George), Reparations Eve.

CHARIOTT walks the streets.

CHARIOTT: Captain's Log. 22:00 hours . . .
The night is cold

I stay in the shadows as I walk the streets
quiet and empty. In the distance
I can hear the—

((Airhorn: BRA BRA BRA BRAAAAH *. . .))*

—like a thousand wails
haunting
out of the domes and stadiums
far away . . .

CBC ANNOUNCER: ((Welcome to the First Annual Reparations Eve Celebration! Bought to you by—*BEEEEP* . . .))

CHARIOTT: Not everybody could get into the celebrations
Proof of screening
glow in the wrist
and you're in.
But I been one of the frozen ones
not frozen as in freezing
frozen like not going nowhere
no work
no travel
no
no
no . . .

BLACKSPACEX RADIO: ((No fear, my frozen ones, your Seer is here . . .))

CHARIOTT: But BlackSpaceX played for the ones
like me who couldn't leave
them who hadda stay close to a spot
or just not get caught.

The sound of a bus approaching, pulling up. SCREECH. *Doors fly open.*

DRIVAH: What you waiting for?

CHARIOTT *stares up at the* DRIVAH *in a red, black, and green cap.*

CHARIOTT: Suddenly remember, I don't know where I'm going. And that curfew's on.

DRIVAH: You coming or nah? Heading north.

CHARIOTT shoots a look over her shoulder.

CHARIOTT: I gotta get off the street, so I jump on.

BANG. Doors close, the bus takes off . . .

TRACK II.

Da bus. Night.

MUSIC is blasting.

CHARIOTT: Inside, the bus is packed! Elder ladies fill the seats. These are the Big Wimmin—*B-Wimmin*—like in their eighties, nineties, wrinkled and ancient. With bright coloured hair, tats, and track suits. Some sleep, others with eyes peeled on old episodes of *Rap City* and *Da Mix* blasting on a screen hung to the ceiling. Everyone joins over the rap proverbs like mantras.

As CHARIOTT moves down the aisle:

B-WIMMIN: *(voices overlapping)* Move nuh!
Can't see!
Chupps
Yo
Move!

CHARIOTT: They wave me "move" 'cause I'm blocking their view. So I squeeze down the aisle—stepping over their bags and Tim boots—to the last empty seat, deep in the back . . .

When I reach, a woman sits on the window side, head deep down in some cooked food, acting like she don't see me.

(to the woman) "Excuse me."

The woman, 'LO, sucks her teeth, annoyed.

(voice-over) She makes a scene of slowly moving her big duffle bags from the seat, stuffs them below between her feet. I sit.

She puts her head back down in her food.

As we drive going through the side streets, she says—

'LO: 'Member, if they ask you
we're just going cross the border, right.
To shop.

CHARIOTT: Cross the border?!

'LO: Yeah, man. Just ovah Brampton.

CHARIOTT: Shit! I can't go over the border! I have to— Drivah! One stop! Driv—

'LO puts down her food—

'LO: Yo! Siddung, guy!

CHARIOTT: Even tho I can't really speak old T-dot
lucky I can understand it
because of my gramma.
So I sit.

'LO brings her voice down, barely makes her lips move.

'LO: We're not really going cross the border, yout'. Relax, eh.

CHARIOTT: You're not?

'LO shakes her head—naaah. Unzips the large bag between her feet and shows CHARIOTT a metal shovel within. She pulls it out and starts to polish it slowly.

'LO: The Land. Ever hear of Ark Nida?

CHARIOTT shakes her head. 'LO gives a cryptic look.

Freedom and a farm. Look it up, still.

B-WIMMIN: F'real.

'LO squints, looks CHARIOTT up and down—like she's seen her before . . .

'LO: Who are you?

CHARIOTT: Chariott.

'LO: Hmph . . . but who you belong to?

CHARIOTT: Ah, nobody.

'LO shakes her head.

'LO: That's not the right answer! . . . Who do you belong to?

Beat. Suddenly CHARIOTT remembers something.

CHARIOTT: Well, my great-gramma was
a Rasta five percenter ancient Kemet-er
Left me a box with scriptures of Yeshua and Queen Afua.

'LO: And who else?

CHARIOTT: My g-mama was a cross between
a sangoma and a hogon
Used to drum for the daughters of Oshun.

B-WIMMIN: True.

CHARIOTT: My mom use to tune into the Church of Coltrane stream
playing St. John

and Alice the god
while she sage-ing the space and running her chunes.

'LO: Like?

CHARIOTT: Hmm . . . Sun Ra. Nipsey. And Roy Ayers's "Daylight."

A little approval in 'LO's side-eye this time.

'LO: N'yeah, eh? Hmph.

B-WIMMIN: Ah ah ah.

SCREECH. The bus slows and jolts to a stop.

CHARIOTT: Red lights flash treacherous through the windows. Outside, the DPs—Drone Police!

DRIVAH looks back through the rear-view, pulls over to the shoulder. As the bus gets quiet—only the sounds of breath . . . Sharp raps on the door.

'LO wields her shovel.

'LO: *(to the B-WIMMIN)* Unnu ready?

B-WIMMIN: Mmhmm!

CHARIOTT: *(voice-over)* The Big Wimmin start to stand and pick up their bags and canes. The woman grabs my arm—and looks at me too.

'LO has a faded barcode on her wrist. CHARIOTT has none.

'LO: Are you?

CHARIOTT: *(voice-over)* I just nod . . . not sure what I'm agreeing to.

'LO whispers—

'LO: Run! To the black hole! Run!

The bus doors fly open.

TRACK III.

The ravine. Night.

CHARIOTT runs!

Sounds of metal hitting metal as the B-WIMMIN fight the DPs.

The high-pitched whine of the DPs whizzing by.

CHARIOTT: So I run
Run I run I run
through the wet and the woods
down the slope cross a stream
I hear the B-Wimmin sing . . .

B-WIMMIN: *(singing to the tune of "Wade in the Water")* Run, girl, run . . .

CHARIOTT: Down into the deep dark of the ravine.

B-WIMMIN: Run, girl, run . . .

The sound of crunching leaves.

CHARIOTT: Feet fly over dead leaves
hands grabbing trees . . .

B-WIMMIN: Run, girl, run . . . *(echoes in the distance)*

CHARIOTT: I trod for kilomiles
Only blinking lights in the sky
filled with satellites to guide . . .

The high-pitched whine of the DP whizzes by. CHARIOTT *freezes. Panicked, she runs, slips, tumbles deeper into the ravine, until . . . she lands at the mouth of a black hole.*

'LO: *(voice-over)* Run! To the black hole! Run!

CHARIOTT *runs inside the black hole to hide.*

TRACK IIII.

The tunnel. Night.

The high-pitched whine fades away.

Breath caught in her chest, CHARIOTT *pants and pants, then—*

SWIING: *(voice-over)* What took you so long?

CHARIOTT *looks up to see a woman in the tunnel—*SWIING.

CHARIOTT: Open my eyes. A woman in front of me, stands in the dark, still as a statue, arms akimbo. Her shadow dances on the walls of the tunnel. She checks me—

SWIING: Belt
Boots
Backpack . . .
Wings.

CHARIOTT: Wings?

SWIING: Hmph, you're not going nowhere without your wings.

CHARIOTT: *(voice-over)* She touches a finger knowingly to her temple. Then she takes off. I run to keep up.

(to SWIING) Why're we in such a hurry?

SWIING: They leaving for Mars tomorrow.

CHARIOTT: Yeah?

SWIING: So we leaving tonight.

CHARIOTT: *(voice-over)* She keeps moving. A flick of light flashes through a crevice in the tunnel walls.

I see then, her feet never meet the ground. I follow the rest of the way in silence
as she coaches me on all I have to know . . .
What to say
and what to play . . .
"Places and Spaces"
"Theme from the Planets"
"Journey in Satchidananda"
in that order . . .

SWIING points to the ground.

SWIING: Watch the rail!

CHARIOTT: *(voice-over)* I step over it, cautious
the electric line between life and death.
She leads me down the centre of the track
till I can see the light at the end.

SWIING turns to CHARIOTT.

SWIING: So, you remember, right?

CHARIOTT: Yes, I remember.

SWIING: You know what to play. Go on.

SWIING gives her a helmet—then raises a hand to her forehead in a stiff salute.

You in the future now.

CHARIOTT: *(voice-over)* Spins on her axis, then she's off, she's gone back down the dark tunnel till she can't be seen.

THE BRIDGE.

A RUMBLE in the tunnel.

On screen: "Black Rocket approaching the station . . . "

CHARIOTT: I jump
from the track to the platform
barely make it before the Black Rocket blazes into the station.

SUBWAY: ((Northbound.))

CHARIOTT: *(voice-over)* It doesn't stop, the doors don't open up. But I hop on!

CHARIOTT leaps in. Three CHIMES as the train moves on . . .

OUTRO.

The train. Night.

CHARIOTT lands in a column of light, and rocks with the rhythm of the train.

SUBWAY: ((Next station.))

CHARIOTT: The train zooms out the underground
All I see is sky
and the whooole city below.

EXPLOSIONS of fireworks!

High over ninety storeys of concrete and glass
topped with 9G towers
Fireworks scar the dark sky with jagged stripes of light.

STATIC—then the sound of the shortwave tuning in . . . CHARIOTT grabs her earlobe in surprise.

BLACKSPACEX RADIO: Happy New Year 2060, my people! It's your astrophonic, dubtronic trip to the Black Galactic. Ricocheting off the ionosphere. Putting the rhythm in your algorithm. This one's for my Afrokinetic Funk Terrestrials. Transmitting from the BlackSpaceX. The last station on your dial. Take a ride, tune in, to the Mothership.

The SFX and voices fuse into a future beat—an epic crescendo.

Altitude—Velocity—Light!

SUBWAY: ((Twenty seconds and counting.))

CHARIOTT: I look around and realize I'm the only one on the train . . .

MISSION CONTROL: ((T-minus fifteen seconds—))

CHARIOTT: I'm going past the last station, going very fast . . .

MISSION CONTROL: ((Eleven, ten, nine . . .))

CHARIOTT: All engines running.

MISSION CONTROL: ((Six, five, four, three . . .))

CHARIOTT: Roaring above the tunnels . . .

MISSION CONTROL: ((Ignition sequence start . . .))

CHARIOTT: Higher than the cloud . . .

MISSION CONTROL & BLACKSPACEX RADIO: ((Guidance is internal.))

CHARIOTT: Roaring thru the sky . . .

MISSION CONTROL: ((We have a liftoff!))

CHARIOTT: At the sound of light!

The RUMBLE *of takeoff.*

Fade to light.

One. Giant. Leap. For. Black. Kind . . .

On screen: One Giant Leap For Black Kind . . .

End.

SEASON 3

Season 3 of *21 Black Futures* was produced by Obsidian Theatre Company and CBC Arts, and was first aired on CBC Gem on February 26, 2021.

Cavities by Adonis Critter King

40 Parsecs and Some Fuel by Omari Newton

The Prescription by Lisa Codrington

Chronologie by Stephie Mazunya, French translation by Tamara Nguyen

Yɛn ara asaase ni by Tawiah M'Carthy

Builders of Nations by Joseph Jomo Pierre

Omega Child by Cherissa Richards

CAVITIES

ADONIS CRITTER KING

Performer: Alison Sealy-Smith
Director: Mumbi Tindyebwa Otu

This play is dedicated to Ambrose and Arwyn. May your water always run clean.

ACKNOWLEDGEMENTS

This play wouldn't be possible without the dedication, talent, and vision of Obsidian Theatre company. Thank you for making *21 Black Futures* a reality. I am so grateful for your trust, generosity, love, and your endless belief in the joys of our Black Future.

I would like to thank my loving partner Nike King, for being the literal Best. Ever! This play wouldn't exist without your love, kindness, revolutionary mind and spirit, and ability to—when I am lying face down on the floor lamenting the written word—cut through my bullshit and get me back on my feet with the gentlest of words. My love, thank you.

Many thanks to Mumbi Tindyebwa Otu for bringing this piece to life!

Thank you, Monica Ogden, Za Hughes, and Karin Saari for your ears, advice, and feedback. And thank you to every revolutionary bad bitch doing the internal work. It ain't easy, but the revolution starts with you.

ABOUT THE PLAYWRIGHT

Adonis Critter King is a multidisciplinary theatre artist, writer, director, and dramaturg. Their arts practice is rooted in social justice as daily practice, revolution as habit that starts in the home, and QT2BIMPOC safe-space curation. Their work uses sci-fi/fantasy, afro-surrealism, memoir, bio-mythology, spirituality, magic, and immersive experience to explore trans identity, the effervescent nature of becoming, and disabled QT2BIMPOC joy, anger, peace, healing, and love. Critter was the 2016 Youth Poet Laureate of Victoria, the 2017 recipient of the Victoria African & Caribbean Cultural Society Community Recognition Award, and in 2020 they received the Witness Legacy Award for Social Purpose and Responsibility Through Art.

ARTIST NOTE

To be at this stage of my life and to be engaging in so many firsts is fantastic: my first time back on a Toronto stage in well over a decade; my first time exploring the theatre-film hybrid space; and my first time working with top-notch talents Mumbi Tindyebwa Otu and Adonis King—it's all intensely exciting! I've been fortunate enough to have been involved in some pretty big things in my time, but to be included in this massively ambitious, totally innovative, future-focused undertaking is the stuff of dreams and a tremendous privilege. It is also hugely personal.

The opportunity to help bring to life Adonis King's evocative, poetic, and powerfully beautiful exploration of legacy, transformation, and the potential for healing could not have come at a more opportune time for me. I am a grandmother, desperately worried about the world my generation is bequeathing my precious grandchildren. Hope is sometimes hard to find. Many days I go to the well, waiting for the wisdom that supposedly comes with age—and choke instead on my seemingly bottomless rage at the willfully myopic, endlessly repetitious injustice of it all. It is almost enough to incite nihilistic despair. Almost. But these are my seeds, my teeth that I have sown, and I owe a responsibility to these future warriors—a responsibility to ensure that in the coming battles there will still, and always, be space for unmitigated, soul-cleansing joy.

Thank you, Adonis, for your visionary words.

Thank you, Mumbi, for so confidently and boldly carrying on the legacy of the Obsidian dream, first birthed twenty-one years ago.

The revolution continues. The future is ours.

—Alison Sealy-Smith, Actor

CHARACTERS

ancestor—Black. has a rotting tooth.

SET

a cracked and scorched earth.
a well.
a thunderous sky.

PROPS

a bag full of teeth.
a heart.
a rotten tooth.

ANCESTOR enters. They carry a large bag and have an aching, rotting tooth. They have been travelling a long time. They take in the well, the cracked and scorched earth, the dark and thunderous sky. They drop their bag.

ANCESTOR: No.
no, no, no, no, no, no, no, no, no,
it isn't supposed to be like this.

we're free!
mama said . . .
nana said . . .

ANCESTOR runs to the well. Tastes it. Gags and spits out the water.

the water is supposed to run clean!
what am i supposed to do with this?
huh?
fuck!

ANCESTOR touches the earth; it is cracked and dry.

more ash than soil.
an impossible task.
an impossible task!

i have given so much of myself!
where does it end?

Thunder rumbles, as if to say, "with them."

ANCESTOR sighs.

yeah.

They go to their bag and pull out many, many teeth. Plants them like seeds.

good luck.
this world sucks.

Thunder rumbles. ANCESTOR *plants a tooth.*

it's gotten better.
revolution's over,
we've won our sweet freedom at last.

ANCESTOR *plants a tooth.*

but we've worked so hard,
scarified so much,
come so far
to still have so much farther to go.

ANCESTOR *plants a tooth.*

i am tired.
angry.
rotten and filthy—

Thunder rumbles. ANCESTOR *sighs.*

but i wish you rest.
ease,
for the rest of your lifetimes.

ANCESTOR *plants a tooth.*

this earth is tough.
i know.
i thought it would be better,
but we've grown through worser stone.

whip, that wove cotton vicious,
colour malicious, bodies promiscuous,
through hate and vain,
we have grown,
and blossomed rage sweet again.

The tooth in ANCESTOR*'s mouth hurts.*

ow!
ugh!

Thunder rumbles.

i didn't ask for this.
nurturing earth with blood and bone
for the last time, planting,
at long last gardening—?
ha!
didn't think i had the disposition for it.

my nana told my mama
"i will do whatever i want to no matter what you say."
which is never what *they'd* say,
so you can see how it's hard to be trusted with this.

ANCESTOR *plants a tooth.*

Beat.

we were never supposed to be free.
remember that.
your life is hard won.
i admit—i have worsened with age,
but you will ripen and flourish
fertilize each day.

you will never know the ways these haunted bones ache,
the way these muscles quake,
only the warmth of our fire,

our rage,
that dawned this new day.

Thunder rumbles.

i have given everything,
and i am tired.
so very tired.

ANCESTOR *finishes planting.*

but i will do what i can, okay?
what i must.

Their tooth hurts again. More than before. Thunder rumbles overhead.

Ow!

ANCESTOR *wipes their hands of dirt. They make to move to the well when their tooth sears, they bowl over in pain.*

OOOOOWWWW!
yes.
okay. okay.
of course.

They reach into their mouth and pull out their rotten tooth. It is black and bloody and angry.

how could i forget about you?
what would we do without you, huh?

They kiss it.

thank you
for getting us here.

They plant it in the earth.

They wipe their hands again and make to go to the well when thunder rumbles overhead and the space in the mouth where their tooth should be sears. ANCESTOR *bowls over and cries out in pain. Stomps their foot.*

Throughout this sequence, using movement/dance and thunder sounds, ANCESTOR *fights their body, which fights to unearth their tooth.*

what?
what more do you want?

Thunder rumbles.

unplant the sun?
ha!
you cannot not make me regret this rage.

Thunder rumbles.

for what?
i am not sorry.
i am not sorry!
i am fury!
i am rage!
healing destructive hurricane,
like mother,
like heavenly father bringing the rain,
i flood this infection out,
end the drought,
and bloom life over again.
like you asked me to.
begged me to
with this gift of survival
over and over again
our sorrow
is etched into my very being—
is it worth nothing?
even now?
even now?

Beat.

what is blacker than rage?
what better honours our pain?

this ache emancipates all we have forgotten,
it is muscle memory. taught and inherited,
gut instinct, unrepented
our history means nothing without it.

without it we cannot survive.

i am begging you,
the rage must be planted
or these children
will never survive.

please!

The body wins and ANCESTOR *pulls out the tooth. The thunder quiets.*

Beat.

then where do i put it?

back inside myself?
this earth
is so selfless and giving,
returned to me barren
yet still births all that will become of me,
endless possibility
reviving.

it can take it.

They go to plant it again. But their hand fights them.

it will destroy me!
devour me from the inside out,

this rage is only meant to be given,
on and on
hand to mouth
i—

Beat.

i see.

ANCESTOR*'s hand goes to their heart. Presses the tooth against it.*

Beat.

i cannot leave you here.

replanted in the children,
they will not inherit this burning chest.
no. they will know peace.

hard earned and done by,
but peace all the same.

Thunder rumbles loud as ever. The clouds are nearly ready to break.

plant peace.

Throughout this sequence, using dance/movement, ANCESTOR *pulls out their still-beating heart.*

i don't know how to do this.
only that i want it.
for you,
for myself
for the soil we owe our wealth.

Beat.

there are so many things to lay to rest.

Beat.

i taught myself to cry.
burned dust from eyes so
grief could defy all that was asked of me.
mother knew, was taught,
this world ain't kind to tha Black chile born sof'
"your tears, queenie, are for tings that matta."

A chuckle, the wry sort. They look at their heart. Their tooth.

tings that matta.

ANCESTOR *moves/dances to the well. Looks inside.*

what will become of me?

Gestures to the planted teeth.

of us?

ANCESTOR *places their heart in the well. They place their rotten tooth into the water.*

Thunder rumbles.

Beat.

we will flourish.

ANCESTOR *starts to pump their heart, like* CPR. *The well water begins to clean, as does the tooth, and* ANCESTOR *exclaims in joy.* ANCESTOR *begins to see the vision, the peaceful future they have planted.*

we will grow sunflower and lily.
oxtail and callaloo,
grits and collard greens,
cornbread cooked both savoury and sweet.

ha!
we will lay to rest in our skin,
settle restless spirits home again,
this temple
will overflow with serenity.

They look up at the swollen sky.

liberation will find me.

They try to drink the water, but it is still dirty. Return to pumping.

on sunday mornings
awoken happy,
entangled limbs, sun kissed—
tastes like coffee.
huh.

They pump faster.

in morning stretches
deep breaths
focus,
recentre back to me,
this life i am living
is gentle,
like cotton used to be.

The water in the well is clearer.

Shift. Through movement/dance or sound effects lighting, as clarity, vision, blessing, settle upon ANCESTOR.

oh, children,
you will no longer know death intimately—
your bodies a prenatal liability.
no, your joy will be limitless,
free.

gap toothed with no apology.
heh.
may i speak candidly?

Beat.

the revolution
is not clean.
it is not kind.
there is bloodshed.
for there has already been so much bloodshed,
wounds echoed for generations—
only to be fixed by taking a knee?
at tha massa's feet?
no.

an eye for an eye was impossible here.

we take everything.

in peace.
like they can't even imagine.

this well is cleaned
by filtering your poison through me
for the last time.

the last time.

Shift.

we take your nation state.
dissolve it into rain.
reinstate indigenous sovereignty,
set every martyr free,
and now,
we will rest.
in safety

at last,
at long last.

liberated.

free.

Blackness, open and loved,
blooming this earth sacred again.

Thunder rumbles.

the end of grief is a beautiful thing.

Clouds burst and it begins to rain. They taste the water but it's still not as good as it could be. ANCESTOR *returns to pumping.*

The teeth begin to grow.

ANCESTOR*'s joy is palpable. They pump and pump and pump until they taste the water. It is drinkable. Clean.*

yes!
yes!

They drink and drink and drink.

And return to pumping.

Blackout.

40 PARSECS AND SOME FUEL

OMARI NEWTON

Performer: Daniel Faraldo
Director: Lucius Dechausay

I would like to dedicate this piece to all Black people that summon the resilience to choose joy in the face of endless aggression. I love you. You matter. We've got this!

ABOUT THE PLAYWRIGHT

Omari Newton is an award-winning professional actor, writer, director, and producer. As a writer, his original hip-hop theatre piece *Sal Capone* received critical acclaim and multiple productions across Canada. Newton's work on Speakeasy Theatre's production of Young Jean Lee's *The Shipment* earned him a 2017–18 Jessie Richardson Award for Outstanding Performance by an Actor, as well as a nomination for Best Direction. Notable film and TV credits include Lucas Ingram on Showcase's *Continuum*, Larry Summers on *Blue Mountain State,* Nate on the animated series *Corner Gas,* Corvus on Netflix's *The Dragon Prince, and* lending his voice to the Black Panther (Marvel) in multiple animated projects. Newton made his Arts Club directorial debut with *No Child* by Nilaja Sun, which ran at the Newmont Stage at the BMO Theatre Centre (Vancouver) September 30 to November 8, 2020. Omari and his wife, playwright Amy Lee Lavoie, received a prestigious Silver Commission from The Arts Club Theatre to co-write *Redbone Coonhound*, a bold and innovative satirical comedy confronting systemic racism, which ran February 17 to March 5, 2023, in the Mainspace at Tarragon Theatre (Toronto).

ARTIST NOTE

The capacity of human innovation is limitless. As a people, we have developed treatments and cures for infectious diseases, created technologies that connect us across time zones, harvested sustainable energy, and explored from the depths of the oceans to beyond the bounds of our own planet. For the most part, if we can dream it, we have found ways to achieve it. But how do you inspire those who refuse, or have forgotten how, to dream? The year is 2050, and despite the progress ignited by the protests and promise of 2020, systemic anti-Black racism remains unsolved.

In *40 Parsecs and Some Fuel*, Satchel Dew is searching for safety in an inherently unsafe place. He has done his best. As an engineer, his greatest invention allows humankind to travel further than ever; he believes somewhere in this galaxy, there is a planet where Black joy can thrive uninterrupted. And instead of spending more energy fighting a system he can never overcome, he's out. He may not get there, and in my mind, even if he does, he only took enough fuel for a one-way trip.

Written by playwright Omari Newton and performed by hip-hop artist Dan-e-o, this is a monodrama that is as intricate in its lyrical wordplay as it is in its ideology. As a father, I spend every day trying to create a better Black future for my kids, and truly—as a closet celestial nerd and huge hip-hop fan—if this place exists and you gotta rhyme your way onto the ship, I might be the first in line. One thing is certain: the capacity for Black innovation and resilience is limitless, and if there is a place for us in this universe, we will find it.

—Lucius Dechausay, Director

CHARACTER

Satchel

The year is 2050. We are inside of a Canadian Military base charged with the design of state-of-the-art vehicles and weapons. Though uncredited publicly, SATCHEL *Dew—a Black man in his mid-thirties—is principal engineer of the* SS *Cole, a groundbreaking space shuttle with the ability to travel to far-off solar systems. We meet our protagonist in the midst of what appears to be an armed hold up. He is executing the true plans for his invention—escaping Earth to find a new planet that is safe for Black people. A planet uncorrupted by white supremacy and colonialism.*

SATCHEL: Apologies for my bluntness but I must make this appeal
My name is Satchel Dew and it's about to get real.
The year is 2050 and I fear it's getting shifty
So I'm here to commandeer a vessel and exit swiftly.

By no means am I a man of means, but I mean you no harm
Many meaner men have made it backed by superficial charm.
With intellect and bootstraps, I scraped my way up the ladder
But in moments you will realize that none of this will matter.

Don't be alarmed, I mean no harm, friend
I'm simply searching for a means to the end.
Of the niggling nagging tapping on the back of my neck
Threading beads of perspiration from my heels to my specs.
Apologies, we've congregated and created technology
So advanced, there's a chance, our work becomes mythology
Of our home and native land, standing on guard
They'll tell the tales of pale soldiers without so much as a shard
Of evidence, that I was relevant to my own creation
Of a shuttle so subtle, groundbreaking for our nation.
Allowing man to boldly go to the previously unseen
The collective culmination of respective hopes and dreams

But my perspective, introspective as it has been,
Has shifted and been gifted with a hunger so keen.
My purpose has surfaced and the vision's crystal clear
I need to speed off in my craft and get the hell up out of here.
We've worked together here, seven years, and things have been fine
Cafeteria serves decent food despite the absence of wine.
My bank account stays fed but my heart starves for respect
And I'm tryna figure out how I can wake up for the next
Alarm clang that sang the song of feeding corporate hogs
Pavlov would applaud of the performance of his black dog
Rise and shine and get in line to punch another clock
Infected like I'm viral, spinning like tick-tock.
'Cause every day I come to work is worse than the last
So every time you see me, my worst day has come to pass.
You can smell the emptiness from underneath my mask
I've reflected on defecting, it's too daunting a task.
Till my breaking point long out of joint has finally been passed.
No matter how this plays out, today will be my last.
As an employee of the State which as of late brings me shame
Today's a chance to cleanse my soul, and clear my good name.
The final straw, the discovery that I have been used
The ship I've built, they'll deploy to destroy my people abused.
So keep your hands where I can see them above your shoulders and shirts
Don't make a move towards the pockets on your jeans or your skirts.
I promise nobody moves and nobody gets hurt
Not on a mission for vengeance just compensation for our worth.

To a Black, female co-worker named Samantha.

Sam,
We've known each other since way back when our mothers
Taught us look out for one another, as a sistah should a brotha.
We were the only brown faces in places where we weren't meant to thrive
It's a miracle the both of us emerged from this alive.
Now we're here as engineers working late for the State that rules
Tasked with masking the rapid diminishment of our nation's fuel.
You have my love and respect and I could never mean you harm
So I plead with you and need you not to pull on that alarm.

40 PARSECS AND SOME FUEL

I'm here to make a proposition that has never been done:
What if we took the tech we've perfected, grab our ship and run.

To a white co-worker named Mike.

Now Mike, you I've never liked, but I'm not one to be petty.
There's no need for me to harm you, but trust that I am ready.
To chop you down like coconuts on the blade of a machete
My cuts will last forever and the blood will flow steady.
If you think to intervene justice will come swift and clean
Just stand aside as Sam and I ride out to pastures green.

To the remaining group of terrified workers at the government military facility.

Racial integration of nations, an experiment that's failed
The galactic exploration tactic will free us from this jail.
With a dream team of supreme engineers who've designed
A shuttle to transport Black folk to the safest land we can find.
So stand me down closely, and know that I'm mostly
Focused as locusts, plaguing all those who don't heed
Our need for an exodus from this godforsaken land.
We need to succeed—this greedy fraud never gave a damn.
See, one can't say they're free when forced to live on bended knee
Or looking over shoulders since we were the age of three.
You proudly knocked down our houses and then erected your own
Then offered us roles in those homes as if we weren't owned.

And see for me the thing that's most grotesque, and even most gory
Is we were not even granted the respect of a story
To justify the lies we're living on any given day
You stayed the course through force and flex it in every single way.
With their violent power they devour our spirit
I've willfully gone deaf because I can no longer hear it
Rather be free and starving than getting paid to be enslaved
So give up the goods, so we bounce and call a spade a spade.

To a Black, female co-worker named Samantha.

Sam, in ways you may have feared me as I had feared you
Afraid that there'd be only one of us they'd let through
Their precision of division to conquer us long term
Keep us focused on the bogus stuff so that we'd never learn
The truth, that we're rooted to upholding this lie
That we were set free, so there is no reason to try.

To a white co-worker named Mike.

So Mike,
Rejoice at the option that we pack our bags and leave
The only thing required is our vehicle to flee
The vessels we've designed to complete the special task
Of seeking a new homeland where Black joy can last
We fought with ferocity, but the atrocities mounted
The monstrosity of the west cannot be discounted.

Face found on the ground, placed down out as we plead.
Sick of the desperate cry, my people still can't breathe.
The future for Black folks must Mark-Us like Garvey
Voluntary separation is needed because we're hardly
Able to table a single day without grief
Tasked with being asked to pledge allegiance to a thief.
In this antiquated system that can't see our worth
We best leave on a shuttle before we leave in a hearse
I've rehearsed this manifesto in my mind many times
Give me freedom or give me death—or leave it all behind.

So Sam, you can join me, hand in hand we can lead
Trust me that there must be life beyond one on our knees
What I'm trying to say cannot be overstated
Further analyzed, minimized, or debated
Our liberation requires full separation
Relocation to nascent nations devoid of latent hatred
Patience was virtuous for four hundred years plus
The immediacy of expediency is a must
My aim may seem insane but I've never had such clarity
We'd be remiss to miss a chance to live in prosperity.

I'm leaving today and if you choose to stay
My final ask is if you pass, you don't stand in my way.

Forty parsecs and some fuel jack
That is the barrier between taking us back
It wasn't you, but you benefit too
From the red white and cruel thugs that stole our souls . . .

The piece ends in a sustained moment of contemplation. We are left to wonder what choice Sam ultimately makes.

End.

THE PRESCRIPTION

LISA CODRINGTON

Performer: Akosua Amo-Adem
Director: Alison Duke

to us

ACKNOWLEDGMENTS

Akosua Amo-Adem, Alison Duke, Sasha Leigh Henry, Myekah Payne, Mumbi Tindyebwa Otu, Luke Reece, Fatuma Adar, Michael Sinclair, Malina Patel and Obsidian Theatre Company, Lucius Dechausay and CBC, and Hughlene and Eileen Codrington.

ABOUT THE PLAYWRIGHT

Lisa Codrington is an actor and writer based in Toronto. Obsidian Theatre Company previously produced her plays *Cast Iron* and *Up the Garden Path*. Lisa has been nominated for three Canadian Screen Awards, the Governor General's Literary Award for Drama, and is a recipient of the K.M. Hunter Theatre Award and the Carol Bolt Award. Other works include *The Adventures of the Black Girl in Her Search for God*, *The Colony*, and *The Aftermath*. Currently, Lisa is working on two new plays and is the facilitator of Obsidian Theatre's Playwrights Unit.

ARTIST NOTE

The year is 2042. There have been technological advances in the field of medicine, especially in the area of mental health and wellness. Recipient 1 is the first to be administered an innovative treatment called Open Your Big Black Mouth. The technology is marketed as the cure for chronic depression and anxiety in Black people overwhelmed by everyday microaggressions, oppression, and anti-Black racism. Never before has a Black woman been given the space to say what's on her mind and not have to deal with white fragility. The monologue follows a skeptical Black woman coming to terms with what this new treatment means for her life. Will it work? What are the side effects? And is she willing to take the risk and accept the consequences?

Directing Lisa Codrington's monologue is a creative highlight for me because it conjures so many emotions that Black women feel today. This is the first time I have worked with text that unapologetically propels an unfettered internal conversation from a Black Canadian woman. It's a tour de force about language that plays with how we receive Black women's stories. What we hear, between what is said and what is not said, is raw and familiar. And I equally enjoyed the process of discovering how deeply we could explore the feelings with actress Akosua Amo-Adem, who is just magical with her delivery. I marvel at how she can bring emotions to life while staying true to Lisa's prose, layered as it is with intricate poetic formations. I have often reflected on what life would be like if I, like Recipient 1, could say what's on my mind about racism, oppression, and sexism, without having to reflect on the consequences. I am drawn to this idea, which is both raw and new.

—Alison Duke, Director

CHARACTER

Recipient 1

Interior. Dosage room—day.

Black.

AUTOMATED COMPUTER VOICE: *(voice-over)* Welcome. Your prescription has been verified. Your treatment begins in five, four, three, two . . .

Lights snap on to reveal . . .

A small room, think Apple-store minimalist. The year is 2042.

RECIPIENT 1—a skeptical Black woman—is in the middle of the room reading the customer information pamphlet for her prescription. Suddenly, a mic rises up from the ground in front of her. She goes back to her pamphlet.

A pamphlet the size of a foldable map, btw. It's covered in fine print and large bolded headings: usage and dosage, warnings and side effects, adverse reactions, dependency and overdose. We catch sight of the headings as RECIPIENT 1 *flips and turns the customer information as she squints to read the info.*

After a moment, she peeks out from behind the pamphlet, eyes the mic, and speaks right to the camera.

RECIPIENT 1: Not just gonna go and take this "treatment" without reading the instructions first.
(re: the mic) Shit like this can go baaaaad. Fast.

Back to customer info.

When I was getting my prescription, I saw a guy picking up his bottle of MMMA mascara.

Pharmacist was showing him how to put it on but . . . the guy was a blinker. Bet he gets an eye infection by the end of the week.

And by the end of the month . . . he'll be lucky if he can see his hand in front of his face to apply the next dose.

Don't get me wrong, I voted for the Marking Misogyny with Mascara Act. I'm happy not to be heckled every time I walk down the street. Problem is, the rate of eye infections in construction workers has created an infrastructure nightmare.

The sidewalks are uneven, our buildings are leanin'—I mean, good luck to those charities working to get waterproof mascara declared a human right. Too little too late if you ask me. Most of those guys got pink eye so bright, they don't even gotta wear orange vests anymore.

So, yeah. I don't know . . .

(re: mic) . . . about this treatment.

Adverse effects could get me, too.

Laryngitis, bronchitis, dry mouth—I'm not 'bout to talk so much that I lose my voice when the whole point of this treatment was to get it back.

My intake officer assures me this is unlikely and encourages me to, "give it a try, just one dose."

> *Lights shift as we get close on* RECIPIENT 1. *She holds up the customer information and delivers the selling points rapid fire.*

(reciting infomercial style) If you're a Black Woman who's been affected by racism, bigotry, microaggressions, white supremacy, exotification, or unwanted hair touching—Open Your Big Black Mouth is for you. Acute or severe, this specially formulated treatment of endless doses of time and space

allows Black Women to speak their mind and be heard. So, go on, girl, open up that Big Black Mouth—dosage as needed.

Pull out as the lights shift back and RECIPIENT 1 *drops the infomercial shtick.*

My intake officer assures me that "this is a lifelong treatment subsidized by the government." "Okay, great," I say, "unless we get a regime change, or another coup and the power swings back to you. What are you gonna do when listening's no longer mandatory and you aren't legislated to?"

Her eyes go wide, her mouth aghast.

And then . . .

BA-BOOM!

That was the first time I ever saw a mind blown. Seen it online (of course) but real life is . . . louder.

Intake officer number two is very concerned that seeing her predecessor BA-BOOMED has traumatized me.

She insists I tell her how I'm *really* feeling. So . . .

I tell her that "I feel like I'm dragging around a sack of my bones. And it's a struggle 'cause I'm starting to crumble and tumble over myself but I continue on because the dragging parts (you know, the parts once restrained in chain) remain intact and determined to contain my pain in this heavy sack. Currently, I'm on the hunt for a back road to ditch this heavy load. So, if you hear of any place . . . "

Eyes wide, mouth aghast.

BA-BOOM!

Never got to add that I've felt this low long, long before I saw her or her predecessor blow.

I did tell her successor, though. Intake officer number three has high, high hopes for me. "With treatment," she tells me, "your success is very, very likely."

But it's hard to alter your route when you're filled to the brim with doubt. Easier to keep on dragging that sack down down the street. In search of a place to chuck and retreat—

Uh oh
another flare
up up
thrown up in the air
to mark the spot
as I make my way down the path to a dark thought.

Beat. RECIPIENT 1 *eyes the mic. Considers . . .*

There is a chance you could be a placebo. An open space where no one hears. Wonder if the illusion I'm being listened to would be enough to replace all my "sack of bones" shit with . . .

Lights shift as we once again get close on RECIPIENT 1 *referring to the customer information. Stock photo images of smiling Black women flash on screen as she runs through the following quotes:*

(reciting testimonial-style)
"I feel like living again."
"I'm happy for the first time."
"I finally know what hope is."

Pull out as the lights shift back.

I'm not an anti-vaxxer.
I understand this is a public health emergency
but see
me
me . . .

I just want to make sure that this shit's been tested properly. 'Cause when it comes to us, care and concern is not always the first order to cross the border.

"But like imagine a world where it is," says intake officer Liz. "Oh, you mean like a world where they run out of numbers and have to turn to names because intake officer after intake officer is going up in flames?"

BA-BOOM!

Who would've thought that your mind could like literally be blown
up up
into the air?

I suppose if you haven't ever had to really listen or think before you speak, when you finally do . . .

> BA-BOOM! *A mind gets blown somewhere outside the dosage room. More follow and continue to build underneath as . . .*

Depending on who you ask, mind-blowing is either the perfect cure for white supremacy or the next public health emergency.

Either way, it's a hell of a mess to clean up. I'd help if I could but we're legislated to take care of ourselves now. And I'm gonna need a little time with the how.

'Cause after hundreds of generations of pleading for our life
for our breath
longing for death.
Running
jumping
pleasing
disappearing—
unless dishes need clearing.
Fearing.
Rearing children that don't belong to us.
Picking your fruit

while dismissing our own pursuit.
Riding in the back of the bus
driving the bus
cleaning the bus
not making a fuss
pretending it's us.
Holding in 'dat RAS 'OLE CUSS DAT WANT TUH BLAST OUT YUH MOUT' AND SHOUT OUT!

Beat. RECIPIENT 1 *catches her breath. The* BA-BOOMING *stops.*

It's a lot. So . . . uh, yeah. I'm gonna take some time to read the fine print.

RECIPIENT 1 *eyes the mic one last time, then goes back to reading the customer information pamphlet. We stay with her as she reads.*

End.

CHRONOLOGIE

STEPHIE MAZUNYA

FRENCH TRANSLATION BY TAMARA NGUYEN

Performer: Sheila Ingabire-Isaro
Rehearsal Director: Katia Café-Fébrissy
Film Director: Mike Payette

This play is dedicated to Shima, Jayson, Jeremy, and Iteka, may you grow up in a world that is kind and safe for Black girls and Black boys. A special thanks to Stéphanie Jasmin and Tamara Nguyen, for their continued support in my growth as an artist. And most importantly, to Mumbi and the Obsidian Theatre Company for propelling me into my writing debut. I am honoured to be part of this anthology and I couldn't have dreamt of a better debut than alongside some of Canada's most remarkable writers.

ABOUT THE PLAYWRIGHT AND TRANSLATOR

Stephie Mazunya is a trilingual and multidisciplinary artist born in Burundi and raised in Ottawa. In 2015 she moved to Montreal to attend the National Theatre School of Canada. Since graduating in 2019, she has worked on various television projects and with a variety of renowned theatre directors, including Stéphanie Jasmin and Denis Marleau in *Soifs Matériaux* (Espace GO and FTA), Sophie Cadieux in *Nassara* (Centre du Théâtre d'Aujourd'hui), and Wajdi Mouawad in *Notre Innocence* (Théâtre de la Colline in Paris). She was nominated for a 2023 Canadian Screen Award for Best Supporting Actress in a Web Series for her role of Fatou in *Moi j'habite nulle part* Season 2. 2021 marked her official debut as a playwright with the play *Chronologie*. She is now working on various writing projects, including *S'enjailler*, which will be presented in April 2024 at Theatre d'Aujourd'hui in Montreal.

Tamara Nguyen (she/her) is a playwright and a dramaturge based in Tiohtià:ke/Montreal. Her play *Légendes de canapé* was directed by Héloïse Desrochers in 2020 at the Théâtre des Béloufilles. In 2023, her play *Bonnes Bonnes*, which she co-wrote with Sophie Gee, was presented at Théâtre Aux Écuries. The same year, her play *Les papillons du littoral* was directed by Claudia Chan Tak at Quai 5160, and her play *La vraisemblable histoire d'Henri VI* was directed by Héloïse Desrochers at the Théâtre des Béloufilles. As a dramaturge, Tamara has worked with Claudia Chan Tak on *Au revoir zébu* presented at La Chapelle in 2022, and with Stephie Mazunya on *S'enjailler*, which will be presented at the Centre du Théâtre d'Aujourd'hui in 2024. Tamara is interested in political satire and how art can slow down the pace of current events to allow for deeper reflection.

ARTIST NOTE

Chronologie traces the intellectual awakening of Muco, a young Burundian-Quebécois writer. A simple, loaded question—"Where are you from?"—sends Muco spiralling through memories as she questions her identity and her legitimacy as a writer. Unable to feel like she belongs anywhere, the young writer seeks out identity through literature—the only place she feels fully at home. In doing so, Muco searches and documents the life inside and outside of her like a scientist looking for truth.

When I was asked to think of the future of Blackness, I immediately thought of my three-year-old niece. I imagined her twenty years from now and reflected on the questions she might be asking herself as a young woman. Would she also have to explain where her parents are from? What space would race and identity play in her everyday life? What books would be instrumental to her intellectual awakening? *Chronologie* allowed me to explore questions that are now relevant to me and will perhaps still be relevant to my niece and her generation. Furthermore, *Chronologie* is a play about immigration as it explores the gap between first- and second-generation immigrants, and their respective relationships to "home."

—Stephie Mazunya, Playwright

CHARACTER

Muco, twenty-three-year-old Burundian woman.

ENGLISH

Interior. Indistinguishable location—night.

Dark room, we see a shadow in which we can distinguish a woman's body. We hear the sound of breathing, not laboured or rushed but . . . proximal, right beside us, then . . . MUCO, *twenty-three-year-old Burundian woman, speaks calmly to herself.*

MUCO: When they asked you to write about where you are from, you couldn't think of anything. You had always been ordinary, no scars of war to show off, no nights where the rebels came to kill your family. It was your mother who sought refuge from her country of birth.

Fade in:

MUCO*'s shadow pierces through the darkness as we continue to hear her voice. We can see the movement of her shadow. She is walking at a slow and steady pace.*

Your mother had arrived here, fleeing from a war you knew nothing about. She told you stories of her life in Burundi, how she grew up eating juicy mangos and climbing trees. She spoke of her love of literature, about the occasional books her father would bring home, having borrowed them from the university where he worked. She particularly enjoyed romantic French novels.

MUCO *continues to pace slowly between the set walls, almost like she is walking in a labyrinth. The light rises gently, a smooth transition as we gradually start to distinguish her face until we can see her entirely . . . the light is a mixture of rich blues and greens that highlight the richness of* MUCO*'s beautiful brown skin. From this point we never lose* MUCO*'s face. When we are not seeing her face we are seeing her reflection through the set.*

She always encouraged you to be proud of your heritage. She made sure your first language was Kirundi and she held the firm opinion that you should marry a Burundian man. That is until you brought one home. He was from a different ethnic group as you. She had not taught you to tell your countrymen apart. That night, she was very quiet at the dinner table. When he left, it was the first time she spoke to you about the ethnic conflicts in her country. She taught you to never trust men that were not from the same ethnic group as you. You kept dating him, but a bitter taste in your mouth from what your mother had told you made it impossible for you to trust him, even though he had never done anything to deceive you.

You had often been surprised at how insistent she was on marriage, it seemed that the men she had loved had all betrayed her. She wanted you to have a daughter, she wanted you to experience what she felt when she gave birth to you. You were her greatest joy.

You imagined her move here, how she must have been the hope of her family. You knew she had lived at her uncle's house upon arriving here. You had often wondered why she had moved out of her uncle's house and why they never spoke again. She said that men from her country never changed. She later told you how her teachers would offer to give her *A's* if she lent them her body for a night or two. You wondered about rape. You wondered if he had forced himself into her body for a night or two.

You wondered if you could write about your first visit to your mother's country. You thought about the girl you met, at the market in Bujumbura, the one who sold tomatoes to pay for her night school, how you admired her devotion, but you knew that even with a university degree, she might never find work. You wished she had gotten the opportunities that were offered to you. You could have easily become a lawyer, but you didn't want to spend all those years in school. You wanted to write about how rich White people liked to ask you with eyes full of pity about where you were from, they always assumed you were Haitian and when you finally told them your mom was from Burundi, you had to explain that it was a small country next to Rwanda. They would often ask you about the Rwandan genocide and make comments on how lucky you were to be here. You were born here so you didn't know how to talk about a genocide that happened in another country, years before you were born.

MUCO is seen through the transparent wall.

As MUCO speaks about the books she loves, her face lights up. An inner smile.

You wanted to write about the boy you met at work, the one who asked you about your background because you had an accent. You were surprised when he knew exactly where Burundi was. He did not ask you whether you were Hutu or Tutsi. He spoke about his love for Chinua Achebe and for the first time you had a conversation about how you felt at home reading Chimamanda Ngozi Adichie's *Americanah*. The ones before had been surprised that they were renowned African authors. You remember asking your university professor if he could include African authors on the World Literature syllabus—how he laughed and said he would have loved to, but there weren't any. When you got home, you sat in front of your computer and, a quick Google search later, found more than a hundred authors. You started reading all of them, from Fatou Diome to Mariama Bâ, and that's when you fell on *Americanah*. The following day, your professor gave you a copy of *Comment faire l'amour avec un nègre sans se fatiguer* as a gift. He gave you that proud and condescending look of whites who know so little about Black authors they assume Haitian and African authors are all the same.

On your second shift with the boy, you knew you could trust him when he told you he had read all Frantz Fanon's books. You almost started picturing dating him. With him, you would not have to explain that you slept with a bonnet. At the end of the shift you told him how you chose the authors you read; you always read Black authors before you read the white authors. You were scared of his reaction, but he laughed. You could now tell him about the white authors you liked. How, like in Kafka's *Metamorphosis*, you felt like an insect in your family. You told him James Joyce's *Portrait of an Artist* made you want to become a writer. Like Dedalus, you had also left religion and family and found a home in literature.

A while after you started dating him, you told him about your writing project. You told him how you thought about writing about the *Black Lives Matter* movement. You told him in confidence how you felt hypocritical grieving Black Americans you had not known, when you had your own people to grieve. You had adopted the apathy of the West that thought war in your mother's country had nothing to do with them.

You wanted to write about Black sisterhood. Your character was going to be named Ncuti. Ncuti was going to call her friend, and in a long monologue she would cry like you did when you watched the shooting of another Black man. She was going to do what you couldn't. She was going to be open about her depression. Talk about her anger towards her mother's country. But she didn't, she couldn't. You couldn't. Instead, you spent three days questioning your legitimacy as a writer. You thought about all the things you could do that would give you a stable income. You thought of doing what your mother had told you. You were going to be a mortgage broker. They made the kind of salary your mother could be proud of.

Light flickers unnoticeably and then increases smoothly and slowly. The flicker is never clearly distinguishable but it's enough to create a sense of tension.

A breath and, like a wave of inner collapse, MUCO*'s submerged. She is some place between dreariness and confusion.*

On the night he called you to break up with you, you folded at the waist as you collapsed on the floor. You said you understood and hung up the phone. You cried all night and thought about calling your mother. You knew she would say "Women like us do not collapse for men. Women who mourn the dead could not mourn exes." But it was the first time you were in love and you couldn't get past it, even though you had known it wouldn't work the first time you met his parents. The way they were so quick on complimenting how intelligent you were. The way they praised your beauty as if to say you were beautiful despite your dark skin. The way they joked about their son bringing home an exotic trophy. As if they knew you were a phase; something he would grow out of.

You thought about calling him a week later when you learned that your mother had passed away in a car accident. You wanted to tell him how ridiculous it was that your mother had survived a war only to die in an accident. You wished your fingers had not remembered his number as quickly as they did. You dialled his number, but couldn't press the call button. Your mother had told you that she wanted to be buried in her village, that in her death she wanted to be close to the ones she had lost. So you sold everything she left you to fly her body back home. At the airport, you sat next to a young girl speaking Kirundi with her mother. You smiled at the young girl, and when she smiled back, you saw the gap in her teeth. She had a gap in her teeth!

Beat.

MUCO has an inner projection of her as a young girl. We should not see a picture of MUCO as a young girl.

MUCO is looking at herself through the reflection of the transparent set wall, or we can see her through the wall.

MUCO is in a state of disbelief and shock. She is still. Not tears, just stillness, then . . . MUCO resumes talking, the words flow through her spontaneously as if she's finding answers with every thought that comes to her.

You had tears in your eyes, when you thought about the gap in your own teeth, the one you begged your mother to have closed, even though she told you that, in her country, it was a symbol of beauty.

As you boarded the plane, the boy sent you a text message. Seated on the plane, you stared at his message for a long time, then you deleted his number and cried. Not because of lost love. But because a young girl with a gap in her teeth reminded you of what you had lost. Your mother was your country. A home you could no longer return to. You wondered if you would one day have a daughter, if she would be asked where she is from, and if she would need to locate Burundi using Rwanda. And if one day she is asked to speak about where she is from, how she might say: "I am a daughter of many countries, born from a mother without a country, whose mother was nostalgic of a country that tried to swallow her."

We can sense a mixture of hope and worry in MUCO. She is not looking directly at the camera.

The light is low and rich colours (green, blue, purple) light up and surround MUCO. The camera's panning slowly around MUCO's face, then . . . MUCO faces the camera surreptitiously and fleetingly and then . . .

Fade to black.

FRANÇAIS

Interior. Indistinguishable location—night.

Dark room; we see a shadow in which we can distinguish a woman's body. We hear the sound of breathing, not labored or rushed but . . . proximal, right beside us, then . . . MUCO, *twenty-three-year-old Burundian woman, speaks calmly to herself.*

MUCO: Quand on t'a demandé de parler de tes origines, tu n'as pas su quoi répondre. Tu t'es toujours trouvée ordinaire; pas de cicatrices de guerre à exhiber, pas de nuit où les rebelles sont venus tuer ta famille. C'est ta mère qui a immigré ici, pour se réfugier du pays qui l'a vue naître.

Fade in:

MUCO*'s shadow pierces through the darkness as we continue to hear her voice. We can see the movement of her shadow. She is walking at a slow and steady pace.*

Ta mère a fui une guerre dont tu ne connaissais rien. Elle t'a raconté des histoires de sa vie au Burundi. Elle avait grandi là-bas en grimpant aux arbres et en mangeant leurs mangues juteuses. Elle t'a aussi raconté son amour pour la littérature, les livres que ton grand-père empruntait et ramenait à la maison de l'université où il travaillait. Ta mère aimait particulièrement les auteurs romantiques français.

MUCO *continues to pace slowly between the set walls, almost like she is walking in a labyrinth. The light rises gently, a smooth transition as we gradually start to distinguish her face until we can see her entirely . . . the light is a mixture of rich blues and greens that highlight the richness of* MUCO*'s beautiful brown skin. From this point we never lose* MUCO*'s face. When we are not seeing her face we are seeing her reflection through the set.*

Elle t'a appris à être fière de ton pays d'origine. La première langue qu'elle t'a apprise était le Kirundi et elle tenait absolument à ce que tu épouses un Burundais. Jusqu'au jour où tu en as ramené un à la maison. Il n'était pas de la même ethnie que toi. Ta mère ne t'avait jamais appris à différencier les hommes de ton pays. Ce soir-là, elle est restée silencieuse à table. Quand il est parti, ta mère t'a parlé des conflits ethniques dans son pays pour la toute première fois. Elle t'a appris à ne jamais faire confiance aux hommes qui n'étaient pas de ton ethnie. Tu as continué à le fréquenter, mais la confiance s'est effritée et le doute t'a rongée, quand bien même il n'avait rien fait pour te décevoir.

Tu as souvent été étonnée par la manière dont ta mère insistait pour que tu te maries. Tous les hommes qu'elle avait aimés semblaient l'avoir trahie. Elle voulait que tu aies une fille, que tu connaisses le bonheur de donner la vie. Tu étais sa plus grande joie.

Tu imagines l'arrivée de ta mère ici. Tu imagines qu'elle a été l'espoir de toute sa famille. À son arrivée, ta mère avait longtemps vécu chez son oncle. Tu t'es souvent demandé pourquoi elle avait déménagé de chez lui et pourquoi ils ne s'étaient jamais plus parlé. Elle t'a dit que les hommes de son pays ne changeaient pas. Là-bas, ses professeurs étaient prêts à lui offrir de bonnes notes en échange de son corps pour une nuit ou deux. Tu as pensé au viol. Tu t'es demandé si ton oncle n'avait pas commis l'innommable.

Tu as voulu écrire sur ta première visite au pays de ta mère; la jeune femme que tu avais rencontrée au marché de Bujumbura où elle vendait des tomates pour payer ses cours. Tu admirais son dévouement, mais tu savais que même avec un diplôme universitaire, elle ne trouverait sans doute jamais de travail. Tu aurais aimé qu'elle ait les mêmes opportunités que toi. Tu aurais aisément pu devenir avocate, mais tu ne voulais pas passer autant d'années sur les bancs de l'école. Tu voulais écrire sur ton identité, tu voulais écrire sur la façon dont les Blancs te demandaient toujours, le regard plein de pitié, d'où tu venais. La plupart d'entre eux pensaient que tu étais Haïtienne. Tu as souvent dû leur expliquer que ta mère était originaire du Burundi, qu'il s'agit d'un petit pays à côté du Rwanda. Alors, ils te questionnaient sur le génocide rwandais et te disaient combien tu étais chanceuse d'être ici. Tu es née ici. Tu ne pouvais donc pas parler d'un génocide survenu ailleurs, plusieurs années avant ta naissance.

MUCO is seen through the transparent wall.

As MUCO speaks about the books she loves, her face lights up. An inner smile.

Tu voulais écrire sur le jeune homme que tu as rencontré au travail, celui qui t'a interrogée sur ton passé parce que tu avais un accent. Tu as été surprise qu'il sache exactement où le Burundi se situait. Il ne t'a pas demandé si tu étais Hutue ou Tutsie. Il t'a parlé de son amour pour Chinua Achebe et pour la première fois, tu as confié à quelqu'un que tu avais trouvé ton pays en lisant *Americanah* de Chimamanda Ngozi Adichie. Ceux à qui tu avais parlé avant avaient été surpris qu'il existe des auteurs africains de renom. Tu te rappelles de ton professeur à l'université à qui tu avais demandé s'il pouvait ajouter des auteurs africains. dans le corpus du cours Littératures du monde; il avait ri, t'avait répondu qu'il en ajouterait s'ils existaient. Ce soir-là, installée devant ton ordinateur, tu en avais trouvé plus de cent sur Google. Tu avais alors commencé à les lire, de Fatou Diome à Mariama Bâ, et c'est là que tu étais tombée sur *Americanah*. Le jour suivant, ton professeur t'avait fait cadeau d'un exemplaire de *Comment faire l'amour avec un nègre sans se fatiguer*. Il t'avait regardé de ce regard fier et condescendant qu'ont les Blancs quand ils croient s'y connaître en littérature noire, même s'ils ne différencient toujours pas les auteurs Haïtiens des auteurs Africains.

Pendant ton deuxième quart de travail avec le jeune homme, tu as compris qu'à lui, tu pouvais faire confiance; il avait lu tous les livres de Frantz Fanon. Tu as presque commencé t'imaginer le fréquenter. À lui, tu n'aurais pas à expliquer pourquoi tu dormais avec un bonnet. À la fin de ton quart, tu lui as parlé de la façon dont tu choisissais les auteurs que tu lisais ; tu lisais d'abord les auteurs racisés avant de lire les auteurs blancs. Tu avais peur de sa réaction, mais il a ri. Tu pouvais donc lui parler des auteurs blancs que tu aimais. Tu lui as raconté que, comme dans *La métamorphose* de Kafka, tu te sentais comme un insecte au sein de ta propre famille. Tu lui as dit que *Le portrait d'un artiste en jeune homme* de James Joyce t'avait donné envie de devenir écrivaine. Comme Dedalus, tu avais laissé de côté religion et famille pour trouver un pays dans la littérature.

Quelque temps après que vous ayez commencé à vous fréquenter, tu lui as parlé de ton projet d'écriture. Tu lui as dit vouloir écrire sur le mouvement Black Lives Matter. Tu lui as confié te sentir hypocrite de pleurer la mort d'Afro-Américains que tu n'avais jamais connus, alors que tu avais encore ton propre peuple à pleurer. Tu avais adopté cette apathie qu'ont les Occidentaux quant aux guerres qui se déroulent dans d'autres pays, quand bien même il s'agissait du pays d'où venait ta mère.

Tu as alors voulu écrire sur la sororité entre femmes noires. Tu aurais nommé ton personnage principal Ncuti. Ncuti aurait appelé son amie et dans un long monologue, elle aurait pleuré comme tu as pleuré quand tu as vu la vidéo d'un autre homme noir tué aux États-Unis. Ncuti aurait fait ce que tu ne pouvais pas faire. Elle aurait parlé de sa dépression et de sa colère contre le pays de sa mère. Mais elle n'a pas pu. Tu n'as pas pu. À la place, tu as passé trois jours à questionner ta légitimité en tant qu'autrice. Tu as pensé à tout ce que tu aurais pu faire pour avoir un revenu stable. Tu as pensé à faire ce que ta mère t'a toujours conseillé de faire, être courtière immobilière. Les courtiers ont un salaire dont ta mère pourrait être fière.

> *Light flickers unnoticeably and then increases smoothly and slowly. The flicker is never clearly distinguishable but it's enough to create a sense of tension.*
>
> *A breath and, like a wave of inner collapse,* MUCO*'s submerged. She is some place between dreariness and confusion.*

La nuit où il t'a appelé pour rompre avec toi, ton corps plié en deux. Tu t'es écroulée sur le sol. Tu lui as dit que tu comprenais et tu as raccroché. Tu as pleuré toute la nuit et tu as voulu appeler ta mère. Tu savais qu'elle te dirait: « Les femmes comme nous ne se plient pas en deux pour les hommes. Les femmes qui pleurent les morts ne peuvent pleurer les ex. » Mais c'était la première fois que tu étais amoureuse et tu ne pouvais pas t'en remettre, même si tu avais su que ça ne durerait pas le jour où tu avais rencontré ses parents. Tu te rappelles qu'ils avaient été prompts à complimenter ton intelligence, à encenser ta beauté comme pour dire que tu étais belle malgré ta peau foncée, à rire de leur fils qui avait ramené à la maison un trophée exotique; comme s'ils savaient que tu n'étais qu'une phase, quelque chose dont il finirait par se lasser.

Tu as pensé l'appeler, une semaine plus tard, quand tu as appris la mort de ta mère dans un accident de voiture. Tu voulais lui dire combien tu trouvais ridicule qu'une femme qui avait survécu à une guerre puisse mourir dans un accident de voiture. Tu aurais voulu que tes doigts ne se rappellent pas aussi rapidement de son numéro. Tu as composé le numéro, mais tu étais incapable d'appuyer sur le bouton d'appel. Ta mère t'avait dit qu'elle voulait être enterrée dans son village, que dans sa tombe, elle voulait être près de tous ceux qu'elle avait perdus. Tu as donc vendu tout ce qu'elle t'avait laissé pour rapatrier son corps. À l'aéroport, tu t'es assise à côté d'une petite fille qui parlait en Kirundi avec sa mère. Tu as souri à la petite fille et quand elle t'a souri, tu as vu l'écart entre ses dents. Elle avait un écart entre ses dents !

Beat.

MUCO has an inner projection of her as a young girl. We should not see a picture of MUCO as a young girl.

MUCO is looking at herself through the reflection of the transparent set wall, or we can see her through the wall.

MUCO is in a state of disbelief and shock. She is still. Not tears, just stillness, then . . . MUCO resumes talking, the words flow through her spontaneously as if she's finding answers with every thought that comes to her.

Tu as eu les larmes aux yeux en pensant à l'écart entre tes propres dents, celui que tu avais supplié ta mère de corriger, même quand elle te disait que dans son pays, c'était un symbole de beauté.

En montant à bord de l'avion, tu as reçu un message du jeune homme. Assise dans l'avion, tu as fixé son message longtemps, puis tu as supprimé son numéro et tu as pleuré. Non pas à cause de l'amour perdu, mais parce qu'une petite fille avec un écart entre les dents t'a rappelé tout ce que tu avais perdu. Ta mère était ton pays dans lequel tu ne pourras plus retourner. Tu t'es demandé si un jour, tu donnerais naissance à une fille, si on lui demanderait d'où elle venait et si elle aurait à localiser le Burundi à partir du Rwanda. Et si on lui demande un jour de parler de ses origines, elle dira peut-être : « Je suis une fille qui porte en elle plusieurs pays, née d'une mère sans pays, et dont la grand-mère était nostalgique d'un pays qui avait voulu l'avaler. »

We can sense a mixture of hope and worry in MUCO. She is not looking directly at the camera.

The light is low and rich colours (green, blue, purple) light up and surround MUCO. *The camera's panning slowly around* MUCO's *face, then . . .* MUCO *faces the camera surreptitiously and fleetingly and then . . .*

Fade to black.

YƐN ARA ASAASE NI

TAWIAH M'CARTHY

Performer: Peter Fernandes
Director: Dorothy A. Atabong

Charlotte Yaa Anibea Mfoafo-M'Carthy, Joycelyn Ama Mfoafo-M'Carthy, and Maud Akua Mfoafo-M'Carthy, Stella Mfoafo-M'Carthy, Florence Afoa Mfoafo-M'Carthy.

ACKNOWLEDGEMENTS

To the women, mothers before and now, who nurture and nurtured. Thank you for being home.

And Obsidian Theatre.

ABOUT THE PLAYWRIGHT

Tawiah M'Carthy is a Ghanaian-born, Toronto-based theatre practitioner, notable as a director, playwright, and performer. Director credits include *Topdog Underdog* (Canadian Stage), *Fairview* (Obsidian Theatre/ Canadian Stage), *Death and the King's Horseman* (Stratford Festival), and *Rihannaboi95* (Young People's Theatre). Playwright/Creator credits include *Maanomaa, My Brother* (Blue Bird Theatre Collective), *Black Boys* (Saga Collectif), and *Obaaberima* (Buddies in Bad Times Theatre). Performer credits include Sizwe in *Sizwe Banzi Is Dead* (Soulpepper Theatre) and Ato in *Body 13* (MTSpace). Tawiah is a co-artistic director of Blue Bird Theatre Collective and has worked with various organizations across Canada including the National Arts Centre and the Shaw Theatre Festival. Tawiah is a multi-Dora Mavor Moore–nominated playwright and performer.

ARTIST NOTE

It is August 1619. A ship carrying enslaved Africans docks at Point Comfort in the British colony of Virginia, now part of the United States, and over twenty Africans from the ship are sold. This was the beginning of American slavery. Over four hundred years later, what would our ancestors who witnessed and suffered the atrocities of slavery say, seeing that much hasn't changed in 2020? History repeats itself; the Black child is still in bondage. The European scramble for Africa (roughly between 1884 and 1914) saw a continent rich in culture and resources invaded, divided, and depleted. The twenty-first century is witnessing another form of colonization: debt-trap diplomacy, where African countries are held hostage financially, with loans they cannot pay. These loans are extended to them by powerful countries with hidden agendas to extract the economic and political concessions necessary to further their strategic aims. The powerful country increases its leverage over the poor nation.

Will the Black child ever break free? What is the future of the Black child?

Fast forward to 2080, in a dystopian world where Ghana is the only utopia. There is a race war in North America. A rich young Black man leads a vessel carrying five hundred thousand refugees to Osu, off the coast of Ghana. It's a time when Mother Africa says *enough is enough!* Africa is for Africans; Blacks for Blacks. A time when the Black child acknowledges self-worth and embraces self-love. A time when the Black child finally breaks free from systemic bondage. In a time when we are all mixed—halves and quarters of various races—who is truly that Black African child able to reclaim the land? I hope you take away from this piece the many critical themes buried within.

—Dorothy A. Atabong, Director

GLOSSARY OF TWI TERMS

Yen Nananom: Our ancestors
Nanahemmaa / Ɔhemmaa akaasa: Queenmother has spoken
Twifo Praso: The land of the Twi people / A town in Ghana that is inhabited by Twi people
Asaase Yaa: Mother Earth
Yen Asaase: Our land
Sunsum: Shadow
Honhom: Spirit
Obibini ba barima: The Blackman's son
Obuasi / Obu-a-si: Underneath the rock / A town in the Ashanti Region in Ghana
Kumasi: The capital town of the Ashanti Region in Ghana
Na wo obibini ba barima: And you, the son of a Blackman
Nana-Ahemmaa mpayinfo: Elderly Queenmothers
Ahemmaa a wodi anim: Leading Queenmothers
Yen ara asaase ahemmaa: Queens of our own native land.
Me Nena, w'ate na me kaa no?: My grandchild, did you hear what I said?
Yɛn ara asaase ni: This is our own native land
Ɛyɛ abɔ den den de ma yɛn: It is a priceless heritage for us
Mogya a nananom hwie gu Nya de to hɔ ma yɛn: Acquired with the shed blood of our ancestors for us
Aduru me ne wo nso so, Sɛ yɛbɛyɛ bi atoa so: It is now our turn to continue what our ancestors started

CHARACTERS

Kobe/Kobena: a young black man in his late twenties. He is mixed. He wakes up at exactly at dawn, every morning. His body knows this now. A soldier's need to be alert. Ready. He wakes up and stands to walk.

That Black Mother/Nanahemaa Akaasa: grandmother to Kobe. They are the head of the 10 Nanahenemaa Payinfo, a revolutionary. They are Ghanaian, an Ashanti mother.

The Rich Chinese Man: the youngest son to an international businessman. He has been there. Done it. Knows it. Always a step ahead. He was born in China.

Interior. Bedroom—dawn (prayer walk for a vision).

KOBE *wakes, rolls out of bed, and stands up. Worshiping, praying in tongues, he walks. His finger tracing the walls of his room, walking the curves and turns, and at dead ends waits for answers until he reaches the centre—the room has slowly transformed into a space, a place. He falls to his knees and opens his eyes to see the 10 Nanahenemaa, led by* THAT BLACK MOTHER.

(Amen).

Interior. Bedroom—home—morning of the gathering.

KOBE: *(robing, preparing, to the gathering)* I have been beating around bushes in my head trying to figure out where to begin.

My mother was half Chinese, half Ghanaian; my father, half Ghanaian, half British. I am a quarter Chinese, a quarter British, and half Ghanaian, all the others, do not count—this time.

I got the call—I have been granted a platform, in the presence of the elders, "Yen Nananom." I called my grandmother, Nanahemaa Akaasa. That Black Mother brought me up from my beginnings. We met at dawn, for a walk in the garden on her estate.

(to the gathering) We talked . . . talked about the first time I left Ghana. I moved with my parents to Canada at fifteen. I came back home at twenty-one during the Race War in North America. I came back for money and . . .

(to THAT BLACK MOTHER*)* You asked me then, whether I wanted my grandfather's money or my mother's inheritance. I chose the money as my resource

and became a Rich Black Man. You told me again how that Rich Chinese made his fortune.

(adorning, preparing, to the gathering) A combination of reality gossip news, hearsay, documented facts translated in That Black Mother's own language . . . my own inherited bias. This is how it goes . . .

Memory—passed-on stories—interior. Living space—daytime.

RICH CHINESE MAN: I am watching "The Grand Tour" hosted by three Rich White Men. They are in Ghana, testing out a Range Rover chassis. They drive from Cape Coast to Kumasi through *Twifo braso*, and make a stop at Obuasi. There, they share with their audience some false British myth about Obuasi and British history in Ghana. One of them finds a quartz rock . . .

The White Man puts the rock in his pocket:

"There is a lot of land here, you should come and buy it, invest in this place, it is the future."

The White Man winks.

I understood what that White Man had said, and I knew I wanted to build something for myself, so I did something.

End of memory.

Interior. Bedroom—home—morning of the gathering.

KOBE: *(adorning, preparing, to the gathering)* My grandfather made it to Obuasi. He paid the town's loans to the region, the region's to the country, and the country's to the bankers. The bankers then paid back "commissions" to the leaders, who picked up their calls. This time, the Rich Chinese Man beat the White Men to the Gold.

He built streets to move the rocks to his ships. The people of Obuasi rejoiced. He built a hospital, and the people of Obuasi rejoiced. Pipes to the waters . . . electricity to operate the mines and the people of Obuasi celebrated him even more—they offered him a stool, and named him a chief.

But the people of Obuasi could not afford the fares for the bus that drove on the tarred road, nor the medications from the hospitals, nor the cost of the electricity. The people of Obuasi were in debt—this time to a Rich Chinese Man. So That Black Mother married him.

My grandmother and my grandfather married in 2028. They needed his money, to play the politics, to regain their birthright . . . so that their children's children's children's children never lack the power and resources to do what needs to be done. Now they are That Black Mother, the holder of all the mining lands in *Twifo braso.*

Pause.

(breathing in, ready) I prayed after my walk with my grandmother and before coming here. I prayed to be welcomed into your presence, into your vision, and in prayer this dawn, I saw something . . .

Into the vision—interior. A space/the void—in the vision.

I am standing on a platform that is floating in a void—no opening or end in sight. Fall, and I will disappear into a further depth below. I see rows and rows of endless contours of glowing—my eyes open more and more—Nananom, Asaase Yaa Henemaa! Their short black hair, illuminating golden halos. Their skin radiating a glorious shine. I see the 10 Nanahenemaa Payinfo, breathing life into this void and Nanahemaa Akaasa, my living grandmother, That Black Mother is one of them. They lead me through the void, threading my life's turns, curves, and dead ends. They draw me into the centre, where the beginnings of life itself exist . . . and right to my memory of their revolutionary speech. Their words come back to me anew.

In the vision—a recorded history revolutionary speech, at the national stadium, to the country, through the screens and all the sound waves.

THAT BLACK MOTHER: Greed and selfishness has brought us here . . . I know not all agree with this revolution—"a reverse of the discrimination that is inflicted on others like us in other places"—and yet when we were there, we fought with them and forgot what was going on, on our own lands.

The rivers and forests that home our ancestral spirits are disappearing. Our gods are being driven away from us again. So much is being taken from our land and not enough given back!

Our charities must begin at home. We have to take back our land to protect it for ours. This land and its resources are not meant for foreigners to pass on to theirs.

For too long our motherland and her children have suffered violence, and the violent take it by force.

We will buy back our lands—its growth and prosperity are dependent on our individual actions. We will pay back every cedi owed from our own pockets.

Ghanafo, this is our own native land, meant for the living bloods of our mothers, it will no longer be owned by those who do not know our gods. We will protect it as a Black Mother protects their own.

End of vision.

At the gathering, interior—coliseum—a sacred space.

KOBE: *(to the gathering)* Yɛn ara asaase ni; Ɛyɛ abɔ den den de ma yɛn, Mogya a nananom hwie gu Nya de to hɔ ma yɛn, Aduru me ne wo nso so, Sɛ yɛbɛyɛ bi atoa so . . .

Nananom, my intention here was to assert my birthright to asaase in *Twifo braso* of Ghana. I thought I understood something, had something, and could do something . . . be something, being who I am.

When I became a Rich Black Man, I built a vessel. At twenty-five, I sailed from Accra to New York, then returned again to Ghana with five-hundred thousand refugees. Nananom, we've been on this shore for a year now, waiting to be let in. I have run out of resources and I have no money of my own. We have been refused landing and none of the ten regions will intercede. You have been bitten once too many times and are twice as shy. The ones on my vessel are all like me—mixed, intersections of halves and quarters of somewhere else.

(to THAT BLACK MOTHER*)* On our walk, this morning, when you spoke. I heard you.

Memory—exterior. Walking in the garden—dawn.

THAT BLACK MOTHER: Me Nena, w'ate na me kaa no?? *[My grandson, did you hear what I said?]* I cannot offer you our land, it is not mine to give away nor yours to offer without asking. We fought for this freedom and we must protect it. Na wo obibini ba barima. *[And you, Black Son.]* What have you done for this land?

End of memory.

At the gathering, interior—coliseum—a sacred space.

KOBE *walks, finding the centre, and he falls to his knees.*

KOBE: *(to the gathering)* Nana-henemaa payinfo, Yen ara asaase henemaa, my blood, my elders, understanding as I do now, I must ask: if not me then who? If not here then where? Where shall we go . . .

Black—the end/the beginning.

BUILDERS OF NATIONS
JOSEPH JOMO PIERRE

Performer: Philip Akin
Director: Kimberley Rampersad

I would like to dedicate this to my parents Cuthbert and Christiana. Also, the most important characters in my life, Sarah, Tyrus, Amiri, and Naliyah.

ACKNOWLEDGEMENTS

I would like to thank Obsidian Theatre Company for having me as part of this collective; Obsidian has been instrumental in my growth as a playwright. When I began Builders it was as a thank you not only to Obsidian but also to my long-time mentor, Philip Akin. Provocative art can in many ways be BUILDERS OF NATIONS.

ABOUT THE PLAYWRIGHT

Joseph Jomo Pierre is an actor and playwright. A graduate of York University's Honours BFA (Theatre), his produced work to date includes *Twisted*, *Shakespeare's Nigga* (2013 Governor General's Literary Award finalist), *Born Ready*, *King ah de Dancehall*, *Pusha-Man*, and *Hip-Hop (Who Stole the Soul)*. In addition to his work in theatre, Joseph has served as consulting director in Allan King's 2006 TIFF documentary, *Empz 4 Life*, which was in part inspired by Joseph's play *Born Ready*. His published works through Playwrights Canada Press include *BeatDown: Three Plays by Joseph Jomo Pierre (2006)*, *Shakespeare's Nigga* (2013), and *Twisted* (2017).

ARTIST NOTE

Creation is an activity not only left for God.

On this earthly plane, the creator is also the artist: man—the one in possession of imagination and the courage to pursue its actualization. Inheriting his father's legacy, Hussein (Philip Akin) takes up his chisel, building upon his inheritance something greater for his son.

Refusing to surrender to the darkness of humankind, Hussein perseveres in the light of those who have gone before him. With a resilient spirit, this Black father shoulders both his responsibility to his legacy and his accountability to the future: not for himself, but for his son, through whom he will find salvation and the reclamation of our nation.

—Kimberley Rampersad, Director

CHARACTER

Hussein

Exterior—day.

HUSSEIN *steps on stage. His face is covered in dust. He is carrying a hammer and a chisel. The hammer is heavy enough to reveal the strain in his forearm. He throws the hammer back, putting his body into a deep arch. Clinching his core, he whips the hammer forward, smashing it into the ground.*

HUSSEIN: "BOOM."

He sits in his silence.

He looks over his shoulder.

You heard that one, Amiri? I said that with my chest. All chest.

He puts his hands on his chest.

I brought the vibrato to the party this time, Amiri.

He smirks.

That's that type of Boom that comes from the loins of God to make the loins of man; that gives you light and darkness, divides water from waters. Watch out, I'll start improvising and give you the Nile, little man.

He laughs.

Listen to me, Amiri: I don't want you coming in here with your youthful swagger, going on about you didn't hear it. I gave you the type of Boom your balls gotta drop to deliver. How your testis hanging?

He chuckles.

How your . . . ha . . . ha.

Motions with his hands.

How low do they go.

He laughs.

You gonna make an old man feel stupid, laughing by himself.

He reflects. In a deliberate manner he picks up the chisel and makes a chiselling motion (this action will be repeated throughout).

Chisel striking stone.

What was the rush, Amiri? Six days does not seem like enough time if you're gonna create a whole world outta nothing. Maybe should have spent the seventh day on us, on man. Grab those moulds of dust, breathe into their nostrils and let them play . . . it wouldn't have taken the entirety of your seventh day to notice the flaws.

He raises his hand.

I can attest; Amiri can attest. We been around them . . . insecurity, jealousy, hate, ain't never been but a breath away.

He kisses his teeth.

Who placing deadlines on you, big fella? Out of whose astrological ass did you pull seven days? We were never perfect. Nobody said you had to stop chipping away.

He exerts his frustration into the strike of the hammer as it hits the chisel.

Chisel striking stone.

The wayward strike causes him to drop the chisel as it stings his hands. Shaking his hands to set the bees free, his gaze rests on a tattoo on the inside of his wrists. It reads "Amiri" with two tiny baby feet outlined in pink and blue.

Kisses his wrist.

For seven months I dreamt you, Amiri. Routinely placed my hands on your mother's belly and closed my eyes. I could see you just swimming around, doing backflips. Maybe, you would swim up and press your little hands and give me a high five. It brought me joy. It was so simple but it brought me joy. Even as the world was already falling around us, I started building a world for you. I started talking to you, out loud. Even when your mother wasn't around. I would speak to you. I would start and finish dishes having told you about history and your future. About Kings and Queens, crowns and thorns, gold and cold iron. I told you how I would protect you. And I know you heard. For seven months I waited for my best friend, the perfect lifelong companion, a better me.

Beat.

When you came. When you came. When you came . . . into this world *(overcome)* . . . you were already out there.

Motions with his hands to the ether.

I held your still body, a seven-month work-in-progress . . . and as each of my breaths, breaths you never took, got shorter and shorter, pushing me to the verge of saying "I can't breathe," I felt you hovering behind me. In a room injected with sudden hysteria and lost faith, as the bowels of your mother's stomach churned out unintelligible tones of anguish, I was calmed by feeling you behind me.

Beat.

Days before the delivery you were already behind me . . . listening to my stories. And now, eighty years later, doing the same. A father never wants to be a burden, and I know I have forced your company, son.

Beat.

How does it feel to be the last man on Earth, to be truly alone? What would keep you going?

Emotionally drained, HUSSEIN *allows his feet to sink into the ground. "How do you know you are truly alone" rattles in his head. Slowly the frames of his last human encounter are pieced together behind closed eyes until it is a complete memory.*

He opens his eyes, picks up the chisel, and strikes the stone—this time with precision.

Chisel striking stone.

HUSSEIN *reins in his focus to what has kept him going these last twenty years.*

Chiselling motion.

Chisel striking stone.

My father told me I was conceived to the words "yes we can." Obama night. The night we got our first Black president. Before that, my father's belief was that it was negligent to bring a Black child into this system. He didn't know if the boogeyman was real, but he felt as if he had seen its shadow. And he couldn't shake that, till Obama night. He said he never saw that coming. And when it came, he didn't understand why that wave never came before. My father always taught me to "walk in your own light"—but he swore he only found his by walking in Barack's. All these Black men hunched over when they enter restaurants, business meetings, could straighten their backs. If you let him tell it, Barack made some white people forget that they were white and just *people*. He personally leaned over and whispered into my father's ear: "Hey, you're *people* too." It's the impact on the soul that creates myths and legends. It was simple representation that gave my father's soul liberation.

So we gotta thank that man. YES WE DO. 'Cause I might not be around otherwise. And we thank all the Black women that let Black men nestle into the warm spot on Obama night. You did a solid; their souls needed that comfort.

Beat.

My father would go to his grave defending that man, building up his myth. He would tell me, "If you let them, they will break the nose off of the Sphinx."

Chiselling motion.

Chisel striking stone.

I been chipping away at this for twenty years. Like the hands that first lashed the rocks of Nubia. Lashed the rocks of Egypt. Lashed the rocks of Meroe. Some days a thousand strikes. Some days two. I've held this hammer in my hand and done nothing but count my breath till the count was lost. I've felt this body get old, alone. I've seen the world die before me.

Beat.

When it came, it went from nobody knowing anybody that had it, to everybody knowing somebody, to somebody being everybody. To nobody left. *The calm was the storm.* You see, when you don't care about one life, or one type of life, it is easy to lose track of the numbers. Till all those ones are the tracks to an old-time train gathering steam, with bellows of death.

Beat.

The problem with man is he became too good at manipulating his environment, too good at winning. So good that he was blinded from his own fragility. Our evolution was no longer in tune with nature. Our evolution was a technological one. The heart had long stopped evolving. But nature never did. She said, "One way or another I'm gonna shoot you fuckas down." "You been way too loud, I can't hear myself." A loud arrogant insecure civilization . . . I could have saved them all, Amiri . . . after your mother died, I tried catching it, but it never stuck to me. For some reason or another it just couldn't. I could have given them this maligned blood and let technology win again. If only I had found one face, one face that told me things would be different. But they are all flawed, Amiri, in ways you never were. I wasn't meant to save them; I was meant to *right* the epilogue. The part of the history that the victor gets to tell. The next go around, we'll start on equal footing.

He blows the dust off of the completed nose of a Barack Obama sphinx.

Thank you for helping me see this through, son. You are free.

He throws the hammer back, putting his body into a deep arch. Clinching his core, he whips the hammer forward, smashing the chisel into his chest.

End.

OMEGA CHILD

CHERISSA RICHARDS

Performer: Emerjade Simms
Director: ahdri zhina mandiela

To my father, Clifford Richards

ABOUT THE PLAYWRIGHT

Cherissa Richards is a playwright, an actor, and a Dora Mavor Moore Award–winning director. Her first play, *Torn Through Time*, a Theatre For Young Audiences production co-written with Frances Koncan and Carrie Costello, was produced at Manitoba Theatre for Young People in 2019 and toured around the province. She is honoured to be part of Obsidian Theatre Company's *21 Black Futures* project. Working with Obsidian always feels like coming home and she couldn't be prouder to contribute this offering for such an inspiring project—lifting up Black voices all across the country!

ARTIST NOTE

The past few years have seen us steadfastly trying to affix "our eyes on the prize": the end of lockdowns, social isolation, physical distancing, and travel restrictions; and much, much, much fewer COVID-19 cases (and Zoom rooms).

And while the now-popular phrases "I Can't Breathe," "Black Lives Matter," "Defund the Police," "End Racism Now," and "Say Her Name" ring on, we want to purge our hearts and minds (and screens) of the whispers and chants and rants that held our gaze. Meanwhile, we mostly continue to ignore the scourge of oppression. We've been looking away from the ravages of racism for hundreds of years despite unending shrieks from the "victims" and "survivors" of this wholly man-made affliction.

If only we could hold our gaze on a future world, like in these few minutes in which Cherissa Richards envisions *Omega Child*. It's a world on the mend, where nature is an underground experience—having been choked by hate, greed, spite, and all other forms of human destruction.

It's a world where ten-year-old Omega—who has never lived on terra firma—and her people hold on to the rites and everyday culture of Black people in the African diaspora. In Cherissa's Black future, Omega conjures her strength to offer a glimpse of both dread and hope; painting vivid colours where monotones want to conquer; spitting rhymes when fear and confusion and desperation set in.

Like in the world of those before her, Omega proffers hope while enduring. "Pour one out for all the homies." Aché.

—ahdri zhina mandiela, Director

CHARACTER

Omega

Exterior. Dark void. Out of time and place.

The screen starts off dark, stark, and empty. As future OMEGA *speaks, use of lights and sound to depict the images described as her words echo into the void.*

OLDER OMEGA: It has been fifty years since our civilization moved underground. We lost so many people in the renegade wars for freedom. We are a few but strong people holding onto our ways, our culture, our Blackness, and our freedom to exist in an oppressive free world.

During the unprecedented, prolonged, and painful fourth term of Agent 45, the Earth descended into chaos. Races clashed and cultures warred. Violence against Black bodies reached astronomical heights of horror.

Blasting sounds of warring armies, faces of Black freedom fighters, explosions and bombs fill the air with an onslaught of sound as lights flash in harried bursts. Projection of war on the backdrop. Images flash in and out throughout the narrator's speech.

An endless stream of murders of our Black brothers and sisters and all people of colour skyrocketed to catastrophic proportions and continued to go unchecked and unanswered for.

Black, Indigenous leaders and people of colour came together to unite and fight against racist splinter groups that were spurned on by 45 and his senseless hate and divisiveness.

But just as we were gaining ground and about to overtake the racist militia groups, Agent 45, in an ultimate fit of delirium and hate, pushed the dreaded red button, setting off a nuclear blast as his last act of defiance. This set off a chain reaction of worldwide nuclear destruction and annihilation.

A projection of an atom bomb mushroom cloud flashes into view in the background, followed by a final resulting loud boom explosion of sound, accentuated with smoke and an orange lighting that fills the stage.

Much of humanity and life across the globe was decimated and vanished in the blast. However, a small, stubborn, and ferocious contingency of Black Militia formed a colony and moved underground to create a stronghold beneath the surface of Earth. This hidden Black community were the last remaining people to survive the blast. These are my people.

As we hid underground, there was talk of a new enemy that emerged. This perilous act of destruction gave birth to an alien invasion. It is said that they had been waiting outside our atmosphere, watching, patiently, for the Earth's inhabitants to destroy themselves: a perfect breeding ground for their attack and takeover. 45's final act of defiance provoked these otherworldly beings into action and now they are said to roam the world.

We lost many people to above ground reconnaissance scavenging missions. So we chose to wait, regroup, and retrain. We waited years, and *this* moment, *now,* is the time to ascend and reclaim the Earth.

A young Black child of ten, dressed in dark camouflage army fatigues, with blacked out goggles and helmet, emerges, wearing an oxygen mask. Carefully, from a mound of debris, she begins to emerge and orient herself, still remaining undercover.

She checks the air quality with her Geiger meter, testing the air's radiation and oxygen levels. It reads: safe. She puts it away in her sac. She cautiously takes off her gas mask.

She breathes this new air for the first time. Small sniffing breaths at first. Taking in how this new air smells. Then larger breaths and finally a deep breath of air. It is a satisfying feeling.

She gasps.

She has company (the audience) and considers them closely. Should she speak to them? She will soon realize innately that they are her inner thoughts, her spirit guides, her conscience, people from the past

. . . a knowing that they are observers that she needs to speak to passes over her.

OMEGA: Hello.

OMEGA is cautious but curious

She holds up her fist in a Black Power sign. She stares the camera, taking in the audience. Can she trust them . . . ? She decides she can.

Shhhh . . . you mustn't speak a word. We must be very quiet. Their hearing is poor, but they sense quick, sharp movements and have very strong sniffers! Their sensors are everywhere—scouting out new bodies to snatch and grab for their alien science experiments.

She stays hidden, too cautious to explore her surroundings just yet.

You might be wondering, "Why did they send me, a child out into such a dangerous world and terrifying mission? Where are the adults? The trained militia? The stealth special ops?"

Well, our wise leaders say the aliens can sense adults no matter where or how they hide above ground—from the scent of their post-pubescent pheromones.

Only the bravest of young children, untouched by "the change," are safe enough to roam the threatening world above.

She takes a step, but a loud gust of wind blows and she jumps back and decides to stay hidden, still too cautious yet to examine the world around her.

I've been training since I was three years old for this mission. They call me *Omega*. I am my people's last hope for survival, the last child born in our underground pod. Many brave kids have come before me, but sadly, many also didn't make it. So it's up to me to be the hope and bring my people a better future!

The Griots—those that keep the stories—say that the blast caused worldwide sterilization, which is why no babies have survived birth since my arrival. Or that the aliens sent a poisonous nerve agent into our underground tunnels to exterminate us or at least stop us from giving birth.

> *She stays under cover, but as the girl speaks (informing the audience), strange lights and sounds pass overhead. The child dodges the sounds and lights, afraid. . . is it aliens or meteor comets that have become natural occurrences from the blast? We don't know . . .*

The Griots tell of a world filled with lush green lands, buildings as tall as the sky, and crystal blue waters—endless colours of a rainbow in a kaleidoscope of dreams. In *my* dreams I fly through the air seeing all these beautiful colours that have returned to the Earth . . . could that really be possible? Imagine all the amazing animals roaming the earth since we left! Maybe even unicorns! Ha!

> OMEGA *stops and listens for any danger nearby, careful not to breathe too loudly.*

My mother died giving birth to me. Papa said I was her last gift to the world. Our supplies are running low, water sources are drying up, and our air systems are failing. My papa lays dying, fighting for breath, and many of our people are gone. It has been so quiet above lately, and the wise leaders say that the alien warlords might have left Earth for other planets. So the time is now!

Don't be afraid!

Papa says:
Lead with love
Big passion
Big heart
Our people's future we do chart!

> *She takes a big breath.*

Here.
I.
Go.

She takes her first steps out of hiding, careful . . . but with every step she is finally exposed to the world around her. As she emerges, a grey light grows and a dreadful sound pulses underneath, revealing the crumbled remnants of buildings and decay. No green. No colour. No hope. No aliens. No nothing. Her little Black body stands there facing upstage. She is merely a dark little shadow in a field of grey debris, a pebble to the giant empty dead abandoned world surrounding her.

She gasps at what she sees. She explores the landscape, looking upstage at the vast emptiness.

Nothing . . . she barely squeaks out of her little dejected voice.

She turns to face the camera, looking at the empty black space in the distance.

No green.
No blue.
No rainbow.
Only grey.
Only . . .
Emptiness . . .

The weight of this realization that humankind has done this to itself overpowers her as she sinks to the ground amidst some rubble. She looks out in total loss and utter hopelessness.

Did humans do this?

Did we do this to ourselves?

OMEGA drops her head, dejected.

She exhales. All of her hope draining from her small body. This crushes OMEGA into tears of deep anguish. It's too much to bear. She cries as the lights darken all around her.

Pause.

A gust of wind blows through the stage and reveals a tiny green bud of a plant and it glows at her feet . . . could it be . . . hope . . . ?

She raises her tear-streaked face slowly to take in this little plant among the vast emptiness. Our little hero breaks into spoken word—inspired from this tiny glimmer of possibility that nature is offering her. She starts to speak slowly, softly at first . . . the rhythm builds.

What?

She can't believe her eyes.

What is this?

She takes a closer look. Are her eyes deceiving her?

Is this even real?

Could it be?

Beat. A tiny light dares to glint in her eye.

Hope?
Is this bud a little symbol of the future—we could cope?
Nah . . .
Can't be.
Don't be a fool.
"You've got a vivid imagination." That's what they're always saying about you.

She chuckles to herself, self-deprecatingly.

You little dope.
It's nothing but crumbled ash and smoke.

OMEGA *looks back at the plant bud.*

Don't let this tiny little thing spin you in a swirl
Of maybe all the happy dreams and possibilities you want
This thing is hopeless

Look around you
It does nothing but to
Haunt—you
Taunt—you
All their stories,
They done got you!

Was it man that perpetrated these atrocities up here?
Maybe there's no UFOs that made the whole world disappear!

What's the message?
What's the purpose?
Who's to blame this fake stuff on?
Does it matter?
Will they shatter?
Do they know it's all just gone?
Must it be that we've succumbed to all this funhouse mirror stuff?
Are we patsies?
Are we dummies?
Giving in to all our fears?

She pauses, considering her people and all she has known before this moment and the lessons she's been taught.

We have grown so very strong in our community below
"Black and Proud" ain't just a mantra—it's a way of life we know
But can we really start anew with just this little glimpse of green?
Do I bring my people up here?
Do I crush their every dream?
Of a future
Of tomorrow
Of a possibility?
Gotta bring them from the bellows
This is a world they *need* to see

OMEGA *returns to the plant.*

If this little tiny herb
Can grow from ashes and scorched earth

Maybe just enough time has passed
For a small chance of rebirth?

Think it's time to call them out here
From the cavernous below
Risk of change must now begin and to start
We must all be in the know.

OMEGA takes a breath. Reciting a type of prayer . . .

Martin, Malcom, Rosa, Trayvon, Sandra, George
The names resound
Pour one out for all the homies
Bring us back this hallowed ground.

OMEGA takes out her flask in a solemn ceremony that is beyond her years and spares one single drop of her precious water to share with the plant.

She smiles at this accomplishment, hope arising within her.

She packs up her flask and makes her way back to where she came from. As she descends back to her people to give them the news, she turns her face to the audience with a wry smile . . . "A new beginning." One last Black Power fist in the air and she disappears.

End.

THANK YOU

CREATIVE TEAM

Set and Costume Designer: Rachel Forbes | Lighting Designer: Shawn Henry | Projection Designers: Cameron Davis and Laura Warren | Props Coordinator: David Hoekstra | Head of Wardrobe: Joyce Padua | Assistant Set and Costume Designer: Jawon Kang | Hair and Makeup Specialist: Bianca Harris

FILM TEAM

Cinematographer: Keenan Lynch | First Assistant Camera: Arvin Cordova | Digital Imaging Technician: Jeff Pentilla | Location Sound Recordist: Kevin Brown | Editors: Ramon Charles, Ashton Lewis, Joe Amio, and March Mercanti | Sound Designer: DJ L'Oqenz | Sound Designers/Mixers: Antoinette Tomlinson, Inaam Haq, Debashis Sinha, and Rez Dahya | Online Editor: Ken Yan | Senior Consulting Online Editor: Jordan Lavigne

PRODUCING TEAM

Artistic Director: Mumbi Tindyebwa Otu | General Manager: Michael Sinclair | Artistic Producer: Fatuma Adar | Company Dramaturge: Myekah Payne | Line Producer: Muzafar Malik | Production Coordinator: Malina Patel | Stage Manager/Script Supervisor: Kat Chin | Production Manager: Crystal Lee | Associate Production Manager: Carlos Varela | Rehearsal Stage Manager: Emilie Aubin | Production Assistant/Driver: Emida Olusegun

ADDITIONAL CREATIVE TEAM MEMBERS

Creative Director: Chinedu Ukabam | Artwork: Yung Yemi | Graphic Design: Gloria Asse Elogo | Publicity: Suzanne Cheriton | Assistant Director: KayGeni (*Jah in the Ever-Expanding Song*) | Assistant Director: Abigail Whitney (*Sensitivity*, *Witness Shift*, *Madness With Rocks*, and *Notice*) | ASL Coach: Natasha "Courage" Bacchus (*Witness Shift*) | ASL Interpreter: Marcia Martins (*Witness Shift* and *Beyere*) | ASL Interpreter: Denica C. Brown (*Beyere*) | Artistic ASL Consultant: Dr. Jenelle Rouse (*Beyere*) | French Dramaturgy: Stéphanie Jasmin (*Chronologie*) | Movement Director: Esie Mensah (*Cavities*) | Workshop Director: Sasha Leigh Henry (*The Prescription*)

CBC

Supervising Producer: Lucius Dechausay | Website: Jeff Hume | Copy Editor: Marcia Chen | Production Manager, CBC Arts: Luke Myers | Manager, Digital Business and Rights: Clara Lee | Executive Producer, CBC Arts: Andrew D'Cruz | Executive in Charge of Programming, CBC Arts: Grazyna Krupa

SPECIAL THANKS TO

BIPOC TV & FILM, Kelly Fyffe-Marshall, Alistair Hepburn, Ravi Jain, Ulla Laidlaw, Weyni Mengesha, Shanna Miller, Jeremy Mimnagh, Charles Officer, Peter Pasy, Ngozi Paul, Trevor Schwellnus, Djanet Sears, and Bahia Watson.

FUNDERS AND SUPPORTERS

Venue Production Partner: TO Live

21 Community Supporters: Harbourfront Theatre, Canadian Stage, National Arts Centre (supporting *Beyere*), Tarragon Theatre, 2b theatre company, BNB Hamilton Fund, Centaur Theatre, Coal Mine Theatre, Crow's Theatre, Downstage Theatre, Eastern Front Theatre, the Musical Stage Company (supporting *40 Parsecs and Some Fuel*), Necessary Angel Theatre Company, Nightwood Theatre, Prairie Theatre Exchange, Royal Manitoba Theatre Centre, Soulpepper Theatre, the Theatre Centre, Theatre Calgary, Why Not Theatre, IATSE Local 58

Obsidian Also Receives Support From: Season Sponsor: TD | Project Sponsor: TAC—Open Door Grant | Sponsors: Canada Council for the Arts, Ontario Arts Council, Toronto Arts Council, Hal Jackman Foundation, and Metcalf Foundation

OBSIDIAN BOARD OF DIRECTORS 2020–2021

Harmony Cohen, Board Chair
Walter Gibbons, Treasurer
Stacey Norton, Secretary
Ashima Chopra, Director
Sascha Cole, Director
Kevin Hanchard, Director
Beverley Thomas-Barnes, Director